Andrew Tidmarsh

Andrew Tidmarsh is a writer, theatre director, film-maker and teacher. Andrew currently works at the Royal Academy of Dramatic Art where he set up the Academy's Foundation course. He also reg   aches at Goldsmiths College, University of London, and was the director of th   luate new-writing festival at Soho Theatre for five years. Andrew has also   e director at Drama Centre London, and has taught at East 15 and the (of Speech and Drama.

As a directo   vorked throughout the UK and also in Germany, Canada, the Philippir   He has made several short films which have been shown at international

For five year   s the acting coach for dancers at the English National Ballet School. He l   esentation coach for various UK companies and has worked with TV pres   iannel 5 and the Discovery Channel.

Dr Tara

Tara Swart   tive performance coach with a background in psychological medicine an   nce. She is an Oxford-trained medical doctor who practised Psychiatry i   Australia and Bermuda for seven years, and has a PhD in neuropharm   ra has numerous publications in journals of neuroscience and coaching.

Tara now ru   n coaching business working with executives, assisting them to maximise th   ial and sustain peak performance. Over the last four years, Tara has worked with companies in the UK, Norway, Sweden, South Africa, the US and China. Her focus in this work is rigorous neuro-psychological techniques. Tara frequently presents at wellness seminars and international conferences.

D1076982

3240

Andrew Tidmarsh and Dr Tara Swart

An Attitude for Acting

How to Survive (and Thrive) as an Actor

NICK HERN BOOKS
London
www.nickhernbooks.co.uk

An Attitude for Acting
first published in Great Britain in 2011
by Nick Hern Books Limited,
14 Larden Road, London W3 7ST

Copyright © 2011 Andrew Tidmarsh and Dr Tara Swart

Andrew Tidmarsh and Dr Tara Swart have asserted their right
to be identified as the authors of this work

Cover design by Peter Bennett

Typeset by Nick Hern Books, London
Printed and bound in Great Britain by
CLE Print Ltd, St Ives, Cambs PE27 3LE

A CIP catalogue record for this book
is available from the British Library

ISBN 978 1 84842 112 7

FSC
www.fsc.org
MIX
From responsible
sources
FSC® C019549

This book is dedicated to all who dare to dream

'Look up to the sky
You'll never find rainbows
If you're looking down.'

Charlie Chaplin
from 'Swing High Little Girl'

Our thanks to Helen Galley, Sue Curnow, Emma Style, Anne Henderson, Alexander Felton, Marek Oravec, Emily Butterfield, Cordelia Galloway, Benjamin Askew, Elizabeth Watkins, Fanny Balcombe, Brigid Panet, Alyssia Kyria, Matt Applewhite and Nick Hern

A.T. & T.S.

Contents

Introduction

The idea for this book came from a conversation. We were talking about how much time is spent looking for work, compared with actually doing it. Tara revealed that for her and her colleagues – executive and business coaches – they spend the vast majority of their working day looking for work: following up on emails, making new contacts or pursuing old ones. For someone working in the arts, this is a revelation. Artists tend to think of themselves differently: they consider the work to be when they are actually creating something, rather than when they are looking for the opportunity to create. When our thoughts turned to actors, it became clear that introducing this almost radical idea could be life-changing. It is clear that a new model is required of how actors view themselves, and how they pursue work. The old model of an actor sitting and waiting for the phone to ring is clearly redundant; we know from talking to many actors that the phone is not ringing. This is what we set out to do in this book: a practical system of exercises and challenges to accompany you in your career. These activities will keep your thinking sharp, your expectations high, and your confidence secure. The fact that you are a talented actor is not something that is under discussion; we assume that you are. The issue, then, is that you are not thinking like a successful actor, and this is the shift in paradigm which needs to be initiated.

Two approaches come together in this book, and in this practice: the science of the brain meets the world of acting. Tara is a medical doctor, neuroscientist and executive coach. Andrew is a theatre and film director, and teacher at UK drama schools. The integration of these two approaches is what makes the book and its suggested methods unique. We hope that the exercises in this book give you a growing sense of core stability: self-awareness, self-confidence and courage. And in turn, the support that this attitude gives will make you strong, active and creative.

We make no promises that reading this book and doing the exercises will lead to fame and fortune. However, we feel confident that reading this book can result in greater happiness, fulfilment, and an increased sense of purpose. We know how it feels when things seem irrevocably bad. The suggestions in this book will help in getting you out of one of those slumps of hopelessness, and also offer a sustainable practice to keep these woes at bay.

Andrew Tidmarsh and Dr Tara Swart

A Useful Attitude 1

As an actor, feelings of powerlessness are an easy option. You often have the impression that you have no control over the path you are taking. Your success and happiness are being prevented by people you do not know and have no way of meeting: agents, casting directors, producers and directors. You are stuck in a cycle of aspiration and disappointment, and each day ends with a dissatisfied feeling of 'if only'.

There is nothing either good or bad, but thinking makes it so.

Hamlet, Act II Scene ii

Let us introduce Lucy. Lucy was thrilled when shortly before her eighteenth birthday she won a place at one of the country's top drama schools. That was five years ago. Lucy enjoyed the first two years of her course. Guest speakers often came in to tell her and her fellow students how hard it was being a professional actor, but Lucy thought that she would be all right. Other people would find it hard: those who are not as talented, or who do not want it as badly. Then, in the final year, she felt that she was not getting the parts in the productions that she deserved. She watched some of her classmates being snapped up by top agents while she was left going for meetings with mediocre agents who did not really excite her. But Lucy signed up with an agent, and, when she first left drama school, she went up for many auditions, but these have slowly decreased in number. Lucy has the feeling that as younger actors have joined the agency, they are now being given the chances that she once had, and her career is being neglected by her agent. Lucy has done some work in the three years since leaving drama school: a national tour of a Jane Austen adaptation, an episode of *Doctors* and a small part in an independent British film. Meanwhile, one of Lucy's classmates is nearly 'A-list'. There are articles about her in gossip columns and photographs of her appear in tabloid newspapers. This classmate has been in a prime-time BBC drama and made two feature films with a major Hollywood film studio. She even occasionally pops up on chat shows. There seems to be 'one' in every year at each reputable drama school: an actor who leaves and goes on to instant film and television success. This seems so unfair.

Lucy feels trapped and unhappy. She recently did a play in a theatre above a pub in North London. She felt that the work was good, but few people came to see it; not even her agent. Lucy got on well with the cast members but few of them had done any paid work at all, and so she felt that they were all a little 'beneath' her in terms of what 'league' they were in. She made a decision that she would never do fringe theatre again, as she felt that doing a 'profit-share' meant that she was making a financial investment herself, as she had to miss work for rehearsals, but still pay her rent and bills. There was clearly not going to be much profit from the profit-share.

Lucy is lucky as she has paid work in a local café. They are flexible with her shifts, so she can get time off for auditions when they occur. She also knows the regular clientele, and so has a sense of belonging, although she gets embarrassed when they ask about her acting career, as she does not seem to have done much lately. Once a week, Lucy helps in a local young persons' drama group. The participants range from eleven to fifteen years old, and they are usually full of enthusiasm. Initially Lucy enjoyed helping out, but now she is feeling tired; tired of keeping other people's dreams alive when hers are fading. In fact, Lucy is thinking about herself less as an actor, and more as a waitress and part-time teacher.

When an audition comes along, Lucy feels so nervous and desperate that she does not enjoy the meeting and is convinced that she does not show herself off at her best. She is beginning to lose her confidence and wonder if she is ever going to act again. Lucy is starting to think that she will give it another twelve months, after which she will put an end to this misery. She has considered training to become a primary-school teacher.

There may be elements of Lucy's story that you recognise:

o   The feelings of hope and enthusiasm you once had when you were younger disappearing.

o   A sense of inevitable disappointment accompanying you most of the day.

o   Looking at successful actors with envy, and questioning why it is them and not you.

o   Feeling frustrated that you do not have the access to the 'gatekeepers' of the industry that others seem to.

o   Feeling that you are spending lots of time thinking about acting, but little time actually doing it.

o   The sense that you are not really an actor any more, but that you define yourself by your part-time job instead.

o   A feeling of anger and bitterness that you are not doing what you want and that you are wasting your life.

Margaret is another actor whose story we will be taking a look at throughout this book. Margaret is at a different stage in her career from Lucy. She once had what she considered to be a successful career. She performed good roles in theatres around the country, and regularly got parts in television dramas. She had performed in all the plays that any actor would hope to do: Shakespeare, Tennessee Williams and Chekhov. These may not have been in theatres in the West End, but Margaret was lucky enough to keep working. Margaret's career took an up-turn and a down-turn simultaneously when she got a recurring part in a long-running television series. Financial reward and everyday recognition were the benefits. The disadvantage occurred to Margaret when the contract ended after two years. Little work then came her way. At this time, Margaret was in her late thirties, and while she had been fortunate and prosperous, her luck and the parts now seemed to be drying up. She had a meeting with her agent, and he told her that he was doing everything he could, but there were fewer parts for a woman of Margaret's age, and she was not getting auditions, even though he was submitting her details. It seemed so unfair because she noticed that there were still plenty of parts for younger women, and that her male contemporaries did not seem to be experiencing this dearth of work even though they too were over thirty-five.

Margaret decided to retrain. She went back to college and refreshed her computer skills and her maths, in addition to doing a course in bookkeeping. Margaret soon found herself to be an office manager at a large national charity. This job led to other positions, and Margaret soon had something that she had never had in her life before – job security. Her agent would phone, and Margaret would find herself unenthusiastic about the roles on offer, and so she eventually reached an agreement with her agent that they would take an indefinite break.

Margaret is now in her late forties, and has not acted for over fifteen years. However, when she goes to the theatre, she recognises a pang deep in her stomach. She feels that she has somehow given up on her ambitions, and there is the nagging accusation in her head that she has somehow betrayed herself.

There are some parts of Margaret's story that you might recognise:

o   A belief that you have failed yourself.

o   The idea that the parts for actors of your demographic are scarce.

o   A feeling that you have been forgotten.

o   A sense that the busiest and happiest times might be behind you.

o   A nagging desire to get back into it, and change everything about your life.

o   A deep feeling of dissatisfaction.

Like Lucy and Margaret, your experiences will form the basis for your beliefs. Therefore, as a result of what you have experienced, this is what you might believe:

o   There is just not enough work out there for actors.

o   Actors with less talent are having more success than you.

o   It is all about whom you know not what you know.

o   Some actors are just lucky.

o   The future is uncertain, but one day you might eventually get what you want.

o   There is nothing you can do.

We have all been in this situation, and thought in this way: seeing external events and other people as the problem; feeling helpless; and becoming consumed with blame and resentment. We feel justified in feeling this because our circumstances support this negativity.

For you, like for Lucy and Margaret, something has to change. You may feel trapped in a cycle of aspiration and disappointment; always holding your breath for a big chance or change in your life. However, the piece of information that you perhaps do not want to hear is that the first thing that needs to change is your attitude.

This next idea might be a difficult one to grasp immediately. You may initially resist accepting it.

You have made friends with this negative thought process. You do not want to give it up. It has become a useful attitude to you.

This attitude of hopelessness has become as reliable and comfortable as an old friend.

Before you read any further do the following exercise:

Exercise: Secondary benefits

Imagine that you have made friends with your attitude of defeat and resentment. Write down a list of all the benefits of keeping this friend close to you. Don't move on until you have done this. Actually write the list down, don't just do it in your head.

Perhaps some of these elements are on your list:

- I don't really have to challenge myself or take responsibility for my situation.
- I rarely have to come out of my comfort zone.
- I can focus on other people and other situations and don't have to spend any time examining myself.

- These feelings of resentment keep my mind busy. It is as if I am full of these feelings and do not have to feel the emptiness of not being successful.

- I have a terrific sense of camaraderie and solidarity with my other friends who are aspiring actors. We can all feel better by moaning about the situation together.

- I find the state of 'limbo' quite comforting. I never have to fully commit to the events of today, as something better will surely come along tomorrow.

These elements lead to inertia and inactivity. This is the path of least resistance, and human beings will always be drawn to this path.

It is important to point out that you have chosen to be an actor. Despite all the warnings about how hard it is, you have chosen to pursue this career. Is there a chance that you actually find the hardship, the waiting, the moaning and the aspiring attractive?

In addition, your life feels stagnant because you are so pre-occupied with the long-term goal that you are neglecting the short-term goals. In short, you have become lost in the fantasy. As a result, you have become unable to take control of reality. For the actor, this is a terrible state to be in. Part of your craft is to portray the everyday responses that an audience can connect with. If you have stopped connecting with the everyday, then there is a chance that your skill as an actor is in jeopardy.

Before you read any further do the following exercise:

Exercise: Reconnecting with what it is that makes you human

Write a list of how you would like your life to be. Do not concentrate on your career aspirations for now; write about the ordinary things – family, house, car, holidays. Be realistic with what you imagine, not fantastic. Don't move on until you have done this. Actually write the list down, don't just do it in your head.

You may have written that you want a mortgage, a flat, a family, a car, good friends around you, a rewarding relationship, and long walks in the countryside. Reflecting on these everyday elements of life will hopefully reinstate a sense of reality, and help you to refocus on what is important from day to day. These are the common desires that unite us all; and by neglecting them, you are failing to connect with living in the present and feeling fulfilled and satisfied.

However, these are the parts of life that take courage and a sense of responsibility. They are the daily commitments which are both banal and extraordinary. Making friends with your sense of defeat, on the other hand, helps you to avoid courage and responsibility, and put off till tomorrow the business of actually taking the first steps. You can feel secure with a childlike sense of not having to commit. The inertia that you are experiencing might be quite appealing, but these ordinary aspirations – house, car, family, etc. – are what most people embrace. They work for them, and this makes them happy. What makes you so different?

Both Lucy and Margaret need to change. Their attitude and way of thinking about life is clearly not helping them. Somehow they need to take back control of their lives. In order to take the first step, there are some things that they need to do immediately. They need to stop:

o   Seeing others' success as the reason for their failure.

o   Blaming others for their situation.

o   Worrying about a lack of security.

o   Judging others by their degree of success.

o   Coming across as desperate.

o   Finding a secret enjoyment when their friends also suffered a lack of success.

o   Talking with their friends about their shared disillusionment and bitterness.

o   Taking everything so personally.

All of these activities lead to inertia and disempowerment.

In order to take back some control, Margaret and Lucy need to replace these activities with other activities to keep busy and prevent these feelings. They need to:

o   Involve themselves with a creative activity daily.

o   Acknowledge that they have made choices leading to feeling stuck.

o   Find the positive elements to their situation.

o   Reassess their core values, so that they see there is more to other people than their apparent success.

o   Develop a realistic long-term overview for their careers.

o   Acknowledge that a sustainable career in acting is built up slowly over many years.

o   Meet like-minded individuals who wish to be creative together.

o   Develop the confidence to approach artists whose work they admire.

o   View themselves as actors even though they are not working regularly.

o   Commit to a daily routine that keeps them in a good working condition.

For Lucy and Margaret, a change is required which affects their very core. They need to start asserting themselves, and this takes courage, imagination and responsibility.

Committing to a healthier attitude takes far more effort and discipline than that of inertia and defeat, and the rewards take longer to realise. There is always the danger that the immediate 'rewards' of being dissatisfied are more appealing.

Every drama school in the country turned me down, and so I was lucky to study drama at all [at Birmingham University]. But even when I came out with my degree, my mother promptly insisted I go straight to secretarial college to have something to fall back on, just in case – which didn't exactly fill me with confidence.

Tamsin Grieg

However, we are not in any way encouraging you to be delusional. We are not suggesting that by following the exercises in this book you will become famous or a global success. We suggest that you will develop a healthier attitude, become more active, and more willing to connect; and be in a position to consider yourself an actor who is ready and able to work.

It is important to ask yourself why you have chosen this particular career path. You have chosen a career in which success appears to be elusive, and you seem stuck in patterns of aspiration and disappointment. So, why then do you want to be an actor?

Exercise: Why acting?

Think about all the positive acting experiences that you have had. Write a list of what it is that acting gives you that no other professional activity can provide. Don't move on until you have done this. Actually write the list down, don't just do it in your head.

Perhaps your list includes the following:

- A chance to be creative.
- A chance to inhabit another person's life.
- A sense of belonging within a company.
- A feeling of success.
- A feeling of being complete.
- A chance to experience heightened emotions in a safe environment.
- A chance to entertain and improve the quality of others' lives.

This is now the challenge: to keep focus on this healthy list of benefits. You have written another list of benefits in this chapter: those benefits of befriending defeat. Reflect on both these lists, and on your list of ordinary pleasures, and remain resolute that you will choose a healthier attitude: one that keeps you focused on your everyday joy, and motivated to think positively. You have a choice between two lifestyles: one will lead to inactivity, deflation and disappointment; while the other will allow you to function effectively, and feel connected and rewarded. It is your responsibility to be clear about the rewards of each lifestyle, and which one you want for yourself.

13

Summary

A defeatist way of thinking can be attractive as it can help you to feel 'comfortable' and included. However, there is another way of thinking about your situation – one which leads to activity, positivity and possibility. Losing sight of the everyday elements of life can be a symptom of this defeatist way of thinking, as you become lost in fantasy. It is up to you whether you welcome dysfunctional inertia or healthy activity. Keeping active requires more effort and focus.

Defeat versus Success

2

Defeating rejection, working with long-term hope, and believing in abundance

A positive frame of mind is especially important when you are having one of those days in which you feel pessimistic, stuck and overwhelmed. It is a good idea, if possible, to focus on hopefulness and a belief in abundance – the idea that there is plenty of opportunity out there for everyone. This will lead to a positive frame of mind, which in turn causes an increased likelihood of positive responses from others. Believing in hope and abundance is nothing more than a state of mind and therefore, as we have already established, a choice. Perhaps self-belief is the key. Self-belief is simply an internal confidence in your abilities combined with a resilience which confirms that you know what you are good at and can cope well, even in the face of adversity. Adversity can come in the form of negative events or critical comments from others. It is not healthy to allow yourself to inhabit communities which are based on negativity; this will not help you build on your belief in yourself.

We were not all born equal in terms of looks, talent, youthfulness, geographical location or wealth. However, if all other factors were equal, the candidate with the sunnier outlook would win every time. This is because it is what people like to be around and what makes the working environment easier. Given the choice, who would *you* rather spend your time with?

Hope, like the gleaming taper's light,
Adorns and cheers our way,
And still, as darker grows the night,
Emits a brighter ray.

Oliver Goldsmith

15

To some extent, positive people are born this way, but social conditioning also plays an important part in terms of expectation and a good sense of entitlement. One of the elements that makes you an adult – in charge of your own life – is that the way you look at things is fully within your control and that of no other.

Andrew: I recently suggested to an actor friend that he might like to meet another friend of mine who is also a successful young actor. Both are young men; both are beginning to establish themselves and develop interesting careers; both are passionate about what they do. I imagined that they would share a sense of humour, and as their casting is so different, neither would feel particularly threatened by the other. I was astonished when, following the suggestion, the first friend replied 'Why would I want to meet him?' I imagine he felt threatened, or he thought that I was implying that this other actor was someone he might look up to. He appeared to be in no mood to meet another actor whose career might be progressing more swiftly than his. I immediately challenged my friend, suggesting that his reaction, while true to his feelings, was immature and that he was missing the point, and missing out on opportunity and possibility.

This anecdote allows us to develop a useful checklist of elements which reveal a poor and ineffective attitude:

o   Are you taking everything too personally?

o   Do you see everyone as competition?

o   Is other people's success painful to you?

o   Are you becoming reluctant to meet new people?

o   Is your prevailing attitude one of bitterness and anger?

Take some time to reflect on which of these you recognise in yourself. There are exercises in the remainder of this chapter to address such issues.

Andrew: I was once passing a film poster with a friend who is an actor. I was astonished by the range of expletives directed at a mainstream actor appearing on the poster about 'Why does she get all the work?' This was a completely unreasonable response. This actor was clearly experiencing a high degree of taking things personally, and had developed an extremely ineffective attitude marked mainly by the degree of bitterness.

Once you start becoming like this, it becomes difficult to change. In short, once you stop believing in abundance and plenty, your very attitude becomes a hindrance to success rather than something that *enables* your success.

The Czech writer Franz Kafka once described impatience as the only crime or sin. For actors, bitterness is the close ally of impatience: an all-pervading and insidious condition which seduces the actor into a state of inertia. One of the main jobs that you have as an actor looking for work is resisting the tendency to become bitter about your situation, and feeling resentment towards those actors who appear more successful than you.

The priority for actors is to ensure that they never become bitter.

Alan David

It is not surprising that bitterness can become a default way of thinking, since actors are forced to confront rejection regularly. It is important to develop your own process for dealing with rejection. By handling rejection in an effective and creative way, bitterness can be kept under control. Try and develop a process which involves the following stages: feel it; accept it; move on and learn from it.

Let us deal with each of these stages individually. The first is: 'feel it'. There is little point in pretending that you are not disappointed. We do not recommend that you simply shrug it off, and pretend that it does not matter. It may matter a great deal, and it is important to face up to how bad it feels. Spend some time with yourself – alone in your room, or out on a walk – and reflect on the disappointment. Give yourself a time limit to sit with the disappointment depending on how extreme it is: an evening, a day, a week. Allow yourself to settle in the sensation for this length of time – listen to moody music, sit in candle-light, watch sad films, go to the cinema during the day, eat chocolate and read magazines. Try and contain this disappointment within yourself; allow yourself to share it with one friend only, to avoid the risk of downward-spiralling into the state of collective bitterness and inertia. In their book *The Art of Possibility*, Rosamund and Benjamin Zander talk about the concept of 'downward-spiralling'.[1] To downward-spiral is to no longer believe in possibility; it is to reduce hope and enthusiasm.

Exercise: A meditation on disappointment

- Sit in a quiet room and allow your body and mind to quieten.

- Reflect on the disappointment that you are experiencing. What is its colour? How does it make you feel about the present time? How does it make you feel about the future? What physical effect is it having on your body?

- Spend a few minutes focusing on these thoughts – allow your body to contain them, and sit with them. Tell yourself that these are feelings that you can manage to contain within yourself; and that it is a feeling that everyone experiences often. This feeling is ordinary.

- Now put this feeling to the side of where you are sitting and imagine it dissolving and sliding away until it disappears.

Repeat this exercise until the feelings of disappointment become less challenging and overwhelming. 'Overwhelm' is another word for what is technically known as stress or anxiety. It is a common experience, and something that we all regularly feel: an inability to function effectively because

---

a particular emotion or thought becomes all-consuming and disproportionately important. With a career full of ups and downs, it is important to recognise when you are feeling overwhelmed, and learn to manage these feelings. Stress and anxiety are described in more detail in Chapter 7.

It will become quicker and easier to accept the truth of the situation once you have developed the habit of feeling disappointment and choosing to let it go. Accept that someone else got the job and the fact that there is nothing you can do to alter it. Use this thought to your advantage: you are now free to do something else. The world of new possibility is opening up to you.

Exercise: Moving on

Take a piece of paper and complete the following two sentences with regard to the disappointment that you were feeling:

1   It is good that I didn't get this job because...

2   Not getting this job has taught me that I need to develop...

When you are thinking about the first sentence, it may be that not getting a job now leaves you free for other possibilities. Take some time to reflect on what these possibilities may be. In the case of the second sentence, what skills or attitudes could have helped you secure the role?

- Better interview technique?

- Better sight-reading skills?

- An ability to appear more confident or more light-hearted?

It is important to remember that getting seen for the part is a triumph in itself. Hundreds of CVs may have been submitted, and you were selected to be seen. This in itself is something positive. You are clearly doing something right. With this knowledge there is now the possibility of further improvement.

Let us return to the anecdote at the beginning of this chapter: the actor who was reluctant to meet another actor as successful as himself. This leads us to two concepts which require some discussion:

o   A shared community.

o   A belief in abundance.

A shared community is an expanded community. In general, people or networks are not something that can be 'stolen'. Most people operate according to principles of generosity, and inclusivity. So, your involvement with another person's network is effectively the merging of two networks. Both groups of people benefit. The actor who showed reluctance and hostility towards the meeting was unaware of how useful the opportunity of sharing contacts, information and experience can be.

Andrew: For several years running, I cast a new-writing festival in London. This was an irksome and tiresome task – often casting up to fifteen plays. When I started, I was dependent on a particular actor to help me to cast it. This actor worked hard to make sure that I had the best possible actors for the roles, and that each new play was served well. After the first year, I became less dependent on this actor. I had made the contacts from the first year, and my network had expanded. However, my deep gratitude for this actor's help in my first year has ensured that I have offered the actor a part in the festival in each subsequent year. I have also recommended him for other work whenever I have had the opportunity.

The dramaturg at the Royal Academy of Dramatic Art is a case in point: Lloyd Trott continues to share his huge network of actors, writers and directors with an exemplary generosity of spirit. People meet each other through play-readings or through his job recommendations. The apparent benefit of this for Lloyd is a connectivity which results in robust optimism, and a joy in his work. He always feels he is part of a community and an ever-expanding network, and this is enough to ward off inertia, bitterness, pettiness and downward-spiralling. Dramaturgs are just as susceptible to these feelings as actors.

The second idea that you need to focus on when you are in a state of bitterness, is that of abundance. When you choose to believe in abundance it is a considerable relief. In the early nineties there was a seminal text by one of the originators of the executive coaching industry: *The Seven Habits of Highly Effective People* by Steven Covey.[2] Although written in the 1990s, this book is still relevant. Covey suggests that one of the habits of highly effective people is a belief in abundance. Whatever it may mean – wealth, work or opportunity – there is enough for everyone. For an actor this is a simple concept: there is enough work, and enough opportunity for everyone who is prepared to put in the effort to get it. This is a belief that should require no proof. Deciding to believe in abundance is a leap of faith. However, the alternative to a belief in abundance is not productive, and can lead to a miserly, bitter and damaging state of mind. It is better to believe in abundance for yourself and for everyone, than to believe that the scarcity of work means that you have to become mean-spirited.

We can hear you protesting at this idea. In the world of theatre, television and film, you might claim, there is simply not enough work to go around. Our response is two-pronged:

o   This is not true.

o   This belief is not serving you.

There is enough work. For the talented, employable and self–motivated actor, there is enough work and enough opportunity. We are not talking about starring roles in Hollywood movies. There is work out there, but you may have to generate the opportunity yourself. As we have stated in the previous chapter, those people who are not working have made a friend of their defeat. They have ceased to believe in abundance; they are not making themselves available for work or opportunity – and as a result they are not working. The belief in a lack of abundance is not serving you; believing in abundance is your only option.

Exercise: Abundance-building

Take a piece of paper and a pencil and make two columns. In the first column write all the feelings that are induced by a lack of abundance. In the second column write how these qualities are transformed by a belief in abundance. For example:

Without abundance	With abundance
Defeat	Possibility of success
Inactivity	Excitement
Panic	Productivity
Disappointment	Optimism
Envy	Openness

Exercise: Barriers to success

- Divide a page into three columns.

- In the first column, list all the barriers in the way of you getting enough of the kind of work that you want.

- In the second column, write the opposite statement. So for example, if you have written 'My agent is not that good' in the first column, write 'I have the best agent in the world' in the second column – not just 'I have a good agent'. Or if you have written 'I am not good-looking enough', write in the second column 'I am the most attractive actor in my age group'.

- Once you have exhausted your list of possible barriers and come up with bold opposite statements, you can start the final column. Write down the answers to 'What I do differently considering that the statements in column two are completely true'. So you do not write 'I *would* get invited to loads of casting meetings', but rather 'I *go* to lots of casting meetings' or 'I get noticed everywhere I go' or 'I win all the romantic lead parts that I go for'. Write down everything you can think of that would be different, even if similar points come up for several of the statements in column two.

- Keep asking yourself if there is anything else until you have exhausted all possibilities. Include 'feeling' statements like 'I am happy and fulfilled' or 'I do not feel the anxiety that I used to'. It is very powerful if, within this exercise, you record these statements as if they are currently true. Look at the list of statements in column three and see if there are any common themes that are showing up and draw coloured circles around the ones that appeal to you most.

When you have completed the previous two exercises, take a look at our suggestions:

- Make a note on four pieces of paper of your (1) physical, (2) mental, (3) emotional and (4) spiritual state when you created the feeling of abundance, and learn how to recreate these feelings for yourself whenever you need to. One way to do this is to lie on the floor or your bed. Remember a time that you genuinely had a success or evidence of abundance and how this changed the way you looked at things. Send a snapshot of this physical, mental, emotional and spiritual state to your brain so that when you are feeling unsettled you can remind yourself of that good feeling – a bit like looking at memorable holiday photos.

- The use of colour for hopefulness – especially yellow or pink ('The future is rosy', 'Looking with rose-tinted spectacles', etc.) can be helpful whether it is the clothes that you wear, a bunch of flowers that you pick and place in a prominent position in your home, the pens or paper that you use to do these exercises, or the food that you eat. Black clothing, although dramatic, can drain you and exude a negative energy. Simply writing lists or doing the drawing exercises in this book with a black or blue pen is not as effective as using a range of coloured felt-tips or crayons to release your inner childlike imagination and creativity.

- Tear off the first of the three columns you wrote at the start of this exercise, scrunch it up and throw it in the bin. Read aloud the statements in column three – hearing your voice making these statements is much more effective than just reading them on the paper, in terms of building self-belief and generating excitement. Commit to doing a number of the things that you have stated as possible over the next few days and weeks.

Barriers	Opposite Statement	What I Do Differently
Not enough time	Plenty of time	Look up what is being cast, write to casting directors and directors
Not enough money	Fabulously rich	Go for a great haircut and get new headshots

If belief in abundance is not your natural way of thinking, or just not the way you have been behaving recently, then it can be a tricky and time-consuming habit to master. To make it a sustainable way of thinking for you, it is best to build it up slowly over time. Use all the techniques described in this book to build a more productive, positive take on things, slowly but surely. Do not rebuke yourself if you lapse into old habits but keep building on your progress. Make sure you do something every day to work towards this way of thinking and being. Most importantly, acknowledge to yourself every day that you have a done a little something to pave the way towards working with long-term hope, and believing in abundance. When these possibilities filter through and you actually start to believe differently, you will notice that you start to behave a little differently, and then that people start to notice. All this compounds your self-belief. It helps, of course, if good things start to happen to build your confidence, but the most successful people are the ones that make this attitudinal shift well before they experience external success factors. Most successful people do not just fall into that situation by luck; they create it for themselves through intelligent effort and determination.

Summary

Taking an attitude of positivity, which includes believing that the right opportunities for you are plentiful, is a matter of choice. Once you have made this decision you can use your positive energy to seek out these opportunities and make them happen. You can also keep a toolkit of strategies for dealing with the inevitable ups and downs along the way. Surrounding yourself with supportive people will enable you to tap into your self-belief to see beyond any immediate barriers.

1 Rosamund Stone Zander and Benjamin Zander, *The Art of Possibility* (Penguin, 2006)

2 Stephen R. Covey, *The Seven Habits of Highly Effective People* (Simon & Schuster, 2004)

Indulgence or Necessity

3

Core beliefs of a successful actor

In this chapter we examine how the way you think about your career may be affecting how open you are to success. One of the main ideas of this book is that you are responsible for creating your own opportunities and success. In order to benefit fully from the chances that come your way, you must be in the right frame of mind: willing, receptive, positive and adventurous. Now, we will look at how you might think that you believe in yourself, but how this belief is only superficial, and how this attitude is hindering your potential for taking control over your career and making real progress.

Part of the difficulty you may be encountering is that of 'deserving'. Perhaps you may regularly encounter some of these thoughts:

o I am the first in my family to want to do this job.

o This job is a hobby, not a profession.

o There are people out there who do really useful jobs like nurses or teachers.

o This is a far-away dream that I will probably never achieve.

It is time to stop these thoughts immediately. If these thoughts cross the mind of successful actors, then they certainly do not linger for very long. The issue of deserving needs to be addressed.

Our doubts are traitors, and make us lose the good we oft might win, by fearing to attempt.

Measure for Measure, Act I, Scene iv

Exercise: Finding the right modal auxiliary

Modal auxiliaries are those little words which modify your verbs:

● I *have to* go now.

● I *need to* get a drink.

Write down some statements about your acting which are true for you. For example:

● I want to act/work.

● I would like to act/work.

● I need to act/work.

● I deserve to act/work.

Look at what you have written. Read it aloud. Now take a red pen and scribble it out. Better still, rip up the list and put it in the bin. This use of these modal auxiliaries simply highlights how you feel about your lack of deserving. These statements emphasise the gap you feel between what you are and how you would like to be. They are defeating you before you start and reveal that, in your mind, the situation is already hopeless. This is affecting the way you react and behave. Everything you do becomes a response to this vast chasm of potential disappointment encapsulated in these words – 'would' or 'want to'. Working actors do not think about themselves in this way. They have managed to fill this void of aspiration by understanding that if the part fits, they deserve it.

Take a piece of paper and write what you are. For example:

● I am an actor.

● I play comedy parts well.

● I perform Shakespeare with clarity.

- I enjoy the creativity of rehearsals.

- I act and I work.

Read these statements aloud, place them somewhere you will see them daily, and start to change the way you talk about yourself to your friends and to people you meet. In fact, the only modal auxiliary that we suggest you use is 'can':

- I can act.

- I can do comedy.

- I can do that part in that film.

A 'can-do' attitude is attractive; it will enable you, and give you a linguistic framework to embody your belief. Our attitudes are revealed by the language we subconsciously choose to use. By consciously changing our language, our negative thought processes may also be changed. This is also true for the statements you have just written and read aloud: by changing how the situation occurs to you, you are changing your behaviour and your response to it. You are building up a core system of belief which will be more permanent. It is also interesting to discover which words contain a negative connotation for you. Is there something taboo about the words *ambition*, *aggressive*, *striving*? By replacing them with less negative words do you generate a more positive response? Do you prefer *focused* to *ambitious*, *determined* to *persistent*; *goal* rather than *dream*? By substituting your taboo words with less emotionally charged words, your aspiration will become less intimidating and your targets more realistic.

In their management book, *The Three Laws of Performance*, Steve Zaffron and Dave Logan go one step further.[1] They suggest that this language is potentially damaging for whole communities, rather than just for the individual:

Most people do not see the potential of generative language because of the all-pervasiveness of descriptive language.

In other words, we are stuck in describing the present: 'It's hard to get meetings'; 'There's no point in doing fringe theatre'; 'My agent is useless.' This is the language that is attractive to us. On the other hand, generative language contains great potential: 'I'm working hard to get meetings'; 'Fringe theatre is rewarding creatively'; 'I'm improving my relationship with my agent.'

Andrew: I have been following the career of a young drama-school student who graduated three or four years ago. He came to see me shortly afterwards because he was feeling lost, disparaged and hopeless. He was not handling the transition from drama school to the world of work. I suggested that he might consider getting a part-time job as a way of feeling more useful or developing a sense of belonging. He pointed out that this was out of the question: he had spent four years training and he was going to act for a living. I remember feeling mildly irritated by this reply as I thought that this young man was refusing to help himself, or take responsibility. But I was wrong, as a few months later he was in rehearsal for something at the National Theatre, and at the time of writing he has worked consistently for the last two years – an extraordinary result.

While this actor's attitude was extreme, and frankly impractical for most of us, it teaches us all something: resolve brings results. This young actor was determined, and his state of distress meant that he was paying the price for his determination. However, his determination did not waver.

I know another young actor who believes the opposite to be true. He might finish shooting a television job on a Sunday evening and on the Monday he will be handing around vol-au-vents at an event with a catering company. For him, inactivity is deadly. He becomes depressed and feels disconnected from his environment. He feels that keeping busy is the key to keeping a healthy attitude.

Even though the approaches of these two actors may seem diametrically opposite, they share the same core belief. They are both consummate actors in that they remain focused on themselves. Each has chosen a strategy to not lose themselves in the banal but necessary world of earning money. If you remember Lucy's story, she works in a café and for a children's theatre class. Perhaps this is not the best way for her to earn money:

o   The emotional investment is high; the work fills her thoughts in her free time.

o   It provides a stable community; she can nest in the security and become too attached to both the people and the support that they provide.

o   It makes her feel validated and needed, something that acting does not, yet the lack of acting deflates her and makes her feel useless.

The distinction here is between someone who is determined to stay active and engaged no matter what he is doing, and someone who is allowing what she has to do to meet her financial requirements sap energy and mental effort from her true purpose and desire.

In one of our workshops we met a successful comedienne who also made ends meet by running an exclusive health and fitness club in central London. She regularly had nightmares about her comedy career making it impossible for her to continue working at the fitness club. She had anxiety thoughts about the business not surviving without her. At the workshop we helped her to make the discovery that her attachment to the gym was preventing her from fully pursuing some of the options which would lead to her success.

Commitment to your career, to your talent and your art is essential. It must be preserved at all costs. If you feel that your sense of identity as an actor is slipping away and you are beginning to see yourself as a teacher, waiter or administrator, then we suggest that it is time for change, and that you work out a way of pre-serving your artistic self.

Andrew: I speak from experience. For three years I didn't direct a single play or short film. I worked as a teacher of English and German at an independent sixth-form college. While I remained frustrated, the school environment provided me with nearly every-thing that I needed: regular income; contact with people; a sense of doing good; a ready-made community. I almost completely for-got about writing or directing. I remember feeling inert, stagnant and dissatisfied. I was unable to kick-start my career and do what I wanted. My original ambition had been overwhelmed by the other benefits of regular work, and I felt unable to take risks. Once I had realised this, I resigned and immediately began to reassess my priorities.

To be eaten does not mean to lose one's identity. Jonah was very much himself even within the belly of the whale.

R.D. Laing

Exercise: Twenty-four hours

Write down your activities in the last twenty-four hours. Don't move on until you have done this. Actually write the list down, don't just do it in your head.

Then, from this list, cross off anything that does not serve your ambition to act or create. What are you left with?

Tara's list:

- Writing this book.
- Listening to music.
- Grocery shopping.
- Viewing two flats.
- Coffee with a friend.
- Attending a weekly business meeting.
- Phoning a friend.
- Watching TV.

- Emailing.
- Preparing slides for a workshop.

In the next twenty-four hours, make sure you do at least one thing that makes you feel like an actor again and nurtures your creativity: a voice warm-up; a movement class; read a play with a friend; arrange to meet a director or an agent; take a singing lesson.

Aim to do one activity every day which nurtures your belief in yourself as an actor. If you can manage it, give yourself one whole day a week to nurture this belief. In an ideal world, you would find a source of income which left every day free for auditions, meetings, classes, reading plays and scripts, and then earn any money that you need in the evening, doing a job that is not all-consuming and does not interfere with your belief that you are an actor. We examine strategies for productivity in more detail in Chapter 4.

When you are feeling low, your resilience in the face of other people's success diminishes. There is a monologue by Steven Berkoff called *Actor*.[2] This reflects how you may feel at times:

> *Hello Peter... How are you?... I'm doing well too... working?... you are?... that's good... Bastard, he couldn't act his way out of a paper bag... the slag...*

Everyone appears to be having better luck, but no one deserves it more than you. It is imperative that you monitor these feelings closely. Bitterness is not helpful. It will make you appear desperate in auditions and dislikeable to people you meet. It is a natural and inevitable emotion, but you must keep it under control.

Some actors' sense of jealousy and entitlement is out of control. They react personally to everything – even the success of international film stars. There is little point comparing your success with that of Colin Firth, Keira Knightley or Cate Blanchett. Your process and development is unique. It is exclusively yours and you can help yourself by owning this process entirely. You will think differently about yourself if you put yourself in a state of mind to celebrate the path that you are on, rather than feel envy for someone else's path.

Incidentally, comparing talent is a completely futile exercise. There is no point in becoming resentful and bitter of others because you consider yourself more talented than them. The world simply does not work that way. We will address this later in the chapter.

Exercise: Appreciation

Part One

Look up a biography of any actor whose success you admire. Spend some time acknowledging what they have done to deserve this success.

For example, following her training at NIDA (the Australian equivalent of RADA), Cate Blanchett spent three years working in theatre in Sydney and winning awards. She then made several Australian TV series, before being cast in the big-budget film *Elizabeth*. It is important to remember that her film success was not instant; preparation and hard work laid the foundations.

Part Two

Examine your own development and growth. Write down three things that you are happy to have learned over the last couple of years, and under what circumstances you have learned them. These things can be professional or personal.

Andrew's list:

- The possibility of collaboration even with difficult people (as a result of my last rehearsal process).

- How to put a proposal together (as a result of not getting a recent directing job, and having to pitch for a new project).

- My skill and confidence working with actors (as a result of the amount of time I have been a teaching director at UK drama schools).

Meditate on this list and celebrate the path that you are on. This list is your reward and is as valuable as fame and fortune, if not more so.

There is a particular phenomenon to watch out for: feelings that swing rapidly between defeat and an overblown sense of entitlement. This instability is symptomatic of bitterness and growing resentment: one minute you think you do not deserve a career and you feel talentless and useless; the next minute you are feeling full of rage and think that everyone else's success should be yours. Actors are quite capable of believing that they are the most talented actor in the world, while simultaneously believing themselves to be completely talentless. This lack of temperance does not help you gain the positive attitude of 'deserving' – this next section is for you.

An essential fact of life

You have a right to create and be creative. Creativity comes in many diverse forms: writing, photography, painting, gardening, knitting... and yes, acting. Being able to look at something at the end of the day and know that you made it is what enriches us as humans. This is what distinguishes us from animals. All cultures in all countries throughout time have believed this and made beautiful art, whether that art is painting, performance or furniture. So why do actors get so stuck and feel so inert and stagnant? There are two chief reasons:

o   Theatre and film are largely transient: they pass, and nothing concrete remains to hold on to apart from the effect that this art has had on us. It can make us wonder exactly what our art and our craft is.

o   Acting, whether in rehearsal or in performance, is a communal activity. On the one hand, you often need someone to act with, and on the other, the performance is only made real by allowing other people – an audience – to witness it.

These two obstacles are where actors often get stuck. The only anti-dote is belief and activity. First, you must believe that you have the right to explore as an artist, and that this requires no justification. Your art happens to be acting – the exploration of stories, relationships and choices. The second thing to do is to take action. There is much that you can do by yourself. We have already mentioned the importance of a daily practice, but what about something more specific to restore your belief in your creativity:

o   Learn and practise a monologue.

o   Pick a character you would really like to play. Write a monologue for that character one year before the play begins.

o   Ask a group of friends to form a play-reading group.

o   Perform some scenes or monologues and video them.

o   Film some sketches or scenes and upload them to the internet, or email them to be watched by your family or friends.

It is only by taking purposeful action that you can build up the belief in yourself as an actor. In this way you can stop yourself from getting stuck, and maintain momentum.

We would suggest keeping either a diary or a blog, and make a commitment to yourself to write in it daily, recording how you have served your craft in the last twenty-four hours, either generally (a voice class or a theatre trip), or more specifically (learning a monologue or recording some scenes). While recording these activities may help you to develop discipline, it is better still that you do these activities because of an intrinsic belief that they will lead you to becoming a better artist.

Perhaps one of the questions that is stopping you from committing to yourself as an actor is whether the job has any value: when all the trappings are stripped away, is it not a selfish and childish job? Well, the pursuit of fame, and the desire to become a star are perhaps childish and selfish, but being an actor is selfless, daring and noble. An actor takes risks and exposes themselves so that the audience may not only be entertained, but also learn about key elements of the human condition: love, loss, abandonment, jealousy, defeat and fear. Often the actor continues to do this despite the fact that the financial reward is minimal and the job security is nil.

> **Exercise: Admiration**
>
> Pick an actor whom you admire. Try and avoid a film star, and think instead of an actor you have seen in a play or an independent film. Write about what this actor gives to the audience. For example:
>
> Mark Rylance is fearlessly willing to show characters that do not fit in to what is considered normal. He is willing to reveal fully the sense of loss and bewilderment at not fitting into the game. He is also willing to show convincingly characters that are unpleasant: narcissistic, violent or manipulative. He does this in such an uncompromising way that his own ego and identity seem to disappear.
>
> Do this exercise with a friend. Discuss actors you admire, and through this positive recognition of what makes them unique as an artist, you will build up your own belief in yourself as an artist.

The acting profession is thousands of years old. Whether it is from Homer, the Old Testament, Norse or Hindu mythology, we have needed stories and storytellers to help us give an order and a framework to the chaos of our daily lives. This is the tradition that actors continue in their work. Storytelling is an essential part of being human: to share experience and help us feel less alone. Whether it is *The Oresteia, Hamlet, Casablanca, Doctor Who* or a devised play in a tiny theatre, their function and purpose is the same. These stories are a source of comfort, and a point of contact for people to explore what it means to be human in this chaotic world. Surely, then, this is a noble and altruistic profession to have chosen, and an essential tradition to serve.

A word of warning. We have just discussed the nobility and beauty of being an actor, and yet it often seems sordid, sullied and petty. When acting becomes competitive, and careers become a race to win, the result is deadly. This form of downward-spiralling may feed your sense of envy and bitterness, but it is destructive to your everyday existence as an actor and those core beliefs that you have been working so hard to build up. Every time you hear yourself saying 'It's all right for them' or 'I could have done it better' or 'If only I had a better agent', you are downward-spiralling, and cutting yourself off from a belief in possibility and abundance. So why do actors like to involve themselves in this activity so much? The answer is simple, and takes us back to our discoveries in the first chapter: your sense of defeat has become your best friend, and this bitterness helps you to feel more intimate with and connected to this best friend. So, here is the challenge from now on: *stop doing it*. Especially, stop doing it with groups of other actors. It is important to recognise how damaging it is to do this. It may be a pleasure, but it is a dark pleasure, and one that should be savoured only very occasionally, if ever. It would be more useful to explore *possibility* with another group of actors; to set up a group of like-minded people who cooperate and collaborate with each other and offer support for each other's hopes and dreams.

I know from my own experience that great films and great actors can have a really big influence on you. There is a place for art in the world, and if you're lucky enough to be good at something and to keep being given work, it's not such a bad thing.

Sally Hawkins

Exercise: Seeking the positive

Going to see a play with friends can often result in a veritable 'bitch-fest', in which every element of the performance is savagely criticised. No matter how much you agree with these negative comments, find something positive about the performance, and let the conversation dwell on it. There must be something to have enjoyed in the production.

You've got to believe you can be a stand-up before you can be a stand-up. You've got to believe you can act before you can act. You've got to believe you can be an astronaut before you can be an astronaut. But you've got to believe.

Eddie Izzard, *Believe: The Eddie Izzard Story*

Andrew: Years of teaching at various drama schools have taught me the value of this exercise. Both students and staff need little encouragement to become hysterical about how terrible a drama-school production or presentation has been. The director has worked hard and the students have worked hard, and this needs to be acknowledged in the first instance. All that negative hysteria reveals is the terror we all have of producing work that is not appreciated, and we want to make ourselves feel better by being one of those dishing it out rather than one of those receiving it.

Comparing talent is a futile activity and can only harm you. We can all think of highly successful actors whom we regard as pretty low on talent. Has our damning opinion made any difference to their employability or income? No. Do they care about our opinion? No. Will your bitterness consume you and make you deeply unhappy unless it is somehow addressed? Yes. People succeed because they are tenacious, reliable and connected. And yes, often they are talented too.

Summary

The beliefs of a working actor are different from those who can only think about success. It is important to develop a core belief in yourself as an artist, and this can only be done through daily exercises and practice. It is essential to honour the path that you are on as an artist, rather than compare yourself to others. This sense of deserving must begin on the inside. Successful people in any environment have an easy relationship with their success; it has an obviousness and an ordinariness – their entitlement to it needs no explanation. Their status, self-worth, actions and beliefs all culminate in success. It is a self-fulfilling prophecy.

1 Steve Zaffron and Dave Logan, *The Three Laws of Performance* (Jossey Bass, 2009)

2 Steven Berkoff, *Plays 2* (Faber and Faber, 1994)

Keeping Productive

4

Practices for a healthy attitude and staying involved with your craft

Often your state of mind is defined by the nature of your routine. It is likely that when you are comfortably busy you feel happy. Perhaps this is why, according to the adage, school days are the happiest days of your life. Often when you are busy, your life has a structure. It is the lack of structure that makes the actor who is looking for work feel vulnerable, disconnected, alienated or ill at ease. You will know that whenever your routine changes you feel a certain degree of stress. This might be the case at Christmas, or when you finish a job, or even when you go away on holiday – you might need one whole week to wind down and adjust to the new routine of being on holiday before you begin to enjoy yourself in the second week. Some people cope with change or stress better than others. Just knowing what your comfort level is can be a helpful start in dealing with stress when change happens. When you are between jobs as an actor, the days can feel long, you can become easily disenchanted, and the lack of routine can become enervating and depressing. This is probably the reason why Margaret, one of our actors from Chapter 1, decided to finally give up acting and enjoy the security of a regular job. Depending on a nine-to-five job to fill her days was much less stressful than having to devise her own autonomous routine, which is much easier said than done.

I think one's feelings waste themselves in words, they ought all to be distilled into actions and into actions which bring results.

Florence Nightingale

You know, there may be periods when you're unemployed. Great. You'll never know what will happen from one minute to the next. Yeah, fabulous. You don't know what money you're going to be making in twenty-five years' time. Yeah, baby! It's like being a gambler, and when I was eighteen, that was music.

Bill Nighy

Motivating yourself daily to adhere to a structured routine requires single-mindedness, but if you can remind yourself of how much more active, focused, optimistic and creative you are when you stick to a daily routine, then there is a greater chance that you will do it every day. In terms of maintaining balance and variety, which can also be very stimulating, the routine does not have to be the same every day and some days can be less structured than others. The main aim is not to allow yourself to fall into a spiral of demotivation and inactivity which is extremely difficult to get out of. It might also be a help to think about 'connectivity'. There is a great deal in this book about making and sustaining connections with other actors, directors and casting directors. Your daily practice is a way of creating and sustaining a connection with *yourself.*

There is plenty of scientific evidence (as well as anecdotal evidence) to suggest that being active early in the day, and for as much of the daylight hours as possible, improves mood, attitude and productivity. The reason for this lies in the way the brain chemicals are released. Basically, there is a little spike of cortisol ('the stress hormone') just after dawn that helps people gather energy to get up for the day, and this is related to the action of melatonin, which regulates your internal sleep-wake cycle in synchrony with the external light-dark cycle. Also serotonin ('the happy chemical') is better maintained in the brain by doing some form of exercise, preferably outdoors, and optimally first thing in the morning – in some cases this is said to be as effective as a low dose of an antidepressant (this is dealt with in greater detail in Chapter 7). So, it is probably best to begin your daily practice early and to embrace a longer day filled with activities that are beneficial for your body and mind, rather than succumbing to lethargy and escapism.

Daily practice

Here are some examples of activities that you might include in your individual daily practice:

o   Practice yoga, stretching, or Pilates.

o   Do some voice work.

o   Read some text aloud, such as poetry or a speech.

o   Swim, run, cycle or simply go for a walk.

o   Play a musical instrument.

o   Revisit some of the statements you wrote in Chapter 1 and remind yourself of why you are an actor.

o   Go online to research upcoming theatre and film productions and make a note of who is casting.

The important element of your daily practice is that you are taking time every day to invest in yourself, and remembering to keep your core skills honed. A daily practice can fuel your belief in yourself as an actor, and, in doing so, keep your attitude and outlook healthy and practicable. We recommend that you do this alone. This time spent with yourself is important; your belief in yourself is a private matter, and it is up to you to reconcile this belief. You must take responsibility for your dreams and find a self-sufficient way of sustaining them. Equally important, however, is maintaining social interaction. Some people can become quite demotivated by spending too much time alone, so make sure you achieve the right balance for you between the above activities and other shared activities, such as:

o   Going to the cinema with a friend and having a healthy discussion.

o   Contacting other actors who might appreciate your company to meet for a catch-up.

o   Going to an exercise class, or jogging with others.

o   Organising a play-reading or singing with a group.

People involved with playing tennis, football, music, dance or even writing find that a daily practice is desirable, or even essential. Therefore it should not be surprising to find actors with the same level of focus and commitment.

There is an additional benefit to keeping a daily practice: you will be ready to work. We all know stories about actors who have not worked for several years and then suddenly find themselves at the National Theatre, or cast in a major television production. Being ready is an essential part of your job, and when you go to a meeting, it is imperative that you appear healthy, fit and prepared, rather than out of sorts and unwell. As an actor, you simply cannot afford to present yourself to the outside world as anything less than well turned out, energetic and focused. However, we all have those days when we just do not feel like doing anything, when everything feels out of control and we just cannot seem to gather the impetus to start anything. To prepare yourself for these days takes a two-pronged strategy – on the one hand, preventative measures and, on the other, tools and techniques to get out of the slump. Do the following exercises to remain proactive during these inevitable days:

Exercise: Examining and managing your energy cycle

Keep a diary of your mood and energy to see if you can identify a pattern which you may be able to pre-empt. If you are female, include your menstrual cycle in this diary. Just noting one or two words a day on a calendar may be enough to identify a pattern. Alternatively you can use a score out of ten to rate each day or part of a day. Tara did this for a few months by just noting down when her energy became really low and she experienced reduced motivation. She realised this was happening for a couple of days roughly every six weeks if she went without a proper break. Sometimes, especially during the winter months, she would actually get ill or feel as if she was coming down with something. (Other people may just feel very tired or irritable.) So she started marking ahead in her diary when this was likely to happen (every six weeks). She would plan to have a couple of days away from her normal routine, and go and stay with friends or family. If that was not possible then she would have a day in town where she went for a long walk by the river and visited an art gallery or had a massage. If you similarly have the occasional 'down' day, try not to check emails or make any work phone calls or even do mundane tasks around the house; instead free yourself from your normal routine and recharge your batteries.

If there was not a natural opportunity coming up for Tara to have a break, then she would pencil one in, no matter how busy she felt she was. Giving priority to rest and recuperation – be it mental or physical – ensures that you are in peak condition for doing the important things you need to do to the best of your abilities. Over time, Tara no longer needed to assign days for this process formally, as she just became more in touch with her energy levels and instinctively knew if it was time for a break, and later even found that she intuitively managed her time in rhythm with her energy. Although there may be times when this is less practical, such as during rehearsals or long runs of a play or filming, simply being aware of your energy cycle will help, even if it is nothing more than ensuring you get a couple of early nights.

Exercise: Golden moments

Make a list of the top five achievements you are most proud of to date, and any comments or feedback you may have received from others about these. Don't move on until you have done this. Actually write the list down, don't just do it in your head. Record how you felt when these events occurred and why they were so satisfying for you – note any common themes to raise your awareness of what you find rewarding. Re-read these when you are feeling down, just to make yourself smile and remind yourself what motivates you.

Exercise: Success story

Keep a running list of things that have gone well for you. Start all the way back in school days – a play you were in, an award you received, a new friend you made, for example – and add to it in chronological order until it is up to date. Keep adding to this list every time something good happens, no matter how small or large. This list is then available to you when things are not going so well.

Exercise: Self-worth

Listen to some music you really like, take a bath, eat your favourite food, or do anything else that you enjoy. Keep a list of the things that you do to treat yourself and which make you feel good about yourself. Don't move on until you have done this. Actually write the list down, don't just do it in your head. Refer back to this list and do some of these things on your bad days to help you get back on track as soon as possible. A favourite DVD or picking up the phone to an old friend are good ideas for these sorts of days.

There are other ways to keep productive in the longer-term. These activities have been categorised into three groups: low-impact, mid-impact and high-impact activities.

Low-impact activities

These are for the days when you are feeling timid or vulnerable as an actor. Those days on which even carrying out the smallest task feels like it will take an overwhelming amount of effort. The aim is that these activities will gently coerce you into once again being able to take sensible and constructive action.

o *Go to the theatre or cinema*
   Take some time to remind yourself why you are in this profession in the first place. Focus on the enjoyment that this experience gives you, and those around you. This is a generous way to think about your career, which should not only be about furthering your own profile but also about giving joy, entertainment and food for thought to others.

o *Read a play*
   This is a simple and gentle way of getting yourself back into gear. Spend some time reading a play that you have been meaning to read for a while. Think about how you might realistically be cast in it. If you have recently enjoyed a piece of new writing at the theatre, check out the playwright's earlier plays. It may be easier to start off by re-reading a play that you know and find easy to get in to. Alternatively, if you want something fresh, why not check out the plays of a playwright whose work you have seen recently and liked.

○ *Look at websites for casting information*
Whether it is www.artsjobs.org.uk or the various subscription websites, spend some time looking at what is casting at the moment and noting down the details of how to apply. (See Appendix A for more ideas.)

○ *Research casting directors*
Look up who cast recent plays, films or television series that you have enjoyed. Make a note of who did the casting and research how to get in touch with them.

○ *Research upcoming projects*
It is relatively easy to find out what film, television and theatre productions are about to be cast. Various publications including *The Stage* and *Broadcast News* list the announcements of new commissions or films and plays about to go into production. Many libraries have a subscription to these publications so you do not even need to buy them yourself. There are also websites which announce what is going into production. Theatres often announce their new season six months ahead of schedule and therefore before they have cast all the shows. (See Appendix A for more information.)

Mid-impact activities

These activities will make you feel more connected to your goals and aims. While they take more energy and focus than the low-impact activities, you will begin to feel that you are making progress and serving your career by creating a little momentum.

○ *Join a class*
There is nothing like an acting class with a teacher you can relate to, and a high standard of participant. This can make you feel alive again, and restore your faith in yourself as an actor. It is beneficial to have a place to go once a week or so where you can actually do what you have trained to do, rather than sit at home and aspire to do it or imagining yourself doing it.

○ *Set up a play-reading group*
Having a group of committed friends who once a week sit around and read a play together will make you feel connected and creative. Like the ever-popular book group, you can read together, and then re-read parts that have impressed you, or even re-read a whole scene with it cast differently. It is an opportunity to then discuss the play, its strengths and weaknesses, and how you relate to the characters. It is a well-known fact that Joss Whedon, the creator of *Buffy*, *Firefly* and *Dollhouse*, had a Shakespeare reading group in his house every Sunday. Little wonder then that his sense of narrative structure is so strong.

○ *Rewrite your CV*
An up-to-date CV that can be quickly attached to an email or popped into an envelope is essential. This is true for all walks of life, and it is no different for actors. Make sure that your CV includes not only your latest work, but any new skills that you have developed and any workshops that you have been on.

○ *Send out your CV to some film schools*
Directors on BA and MA film-making courses are sometimes not aware of where to get their actors from, and often they are so fixated with the technical

side that they neglect to invest time in finding suitable actors. Perhaps this is why short films from graduating directors or writers are sometimes so poor. You can make it easy for these film-makers by sending them your CV – and even your friends' CVs – so that they have actors on tap. In return you will have the experience of working on camera, and also a few clips for your showreel.

○ *Make a voice-reel/get your showreel edited*
A punchy voice-reel or showreel is essential. There is no reason at all why you should not shoot material especially for your showreel. Think carefully about the material you put on your reels and make sure it represents you in an accurate and marketable way. (See Appendix B for more information.)

○ *Get new headshots*
Ask yourself if your headshots represent you in the most advantageous way. If you have lost weight or put on weight, changed your hair or even (dare we mention it) look older, it is important that you have new shots done so that you actually look like the photographs that are sent out to people. Use a recommendation when choosing your photographer, or pick a photographer whose work you have seen plenty of examples of, and whose style you like. (See Appendix B for more information.)

○ *Have a singing or voice lesson*
Honing one of your fundamental skills will make you feel like an actor again. It is always good to check in with a teacher that you trust to see what vocal habits have been unconsciously developing. Also, any new exercises that you learn will help to keep your daily practice fresh and interesting.

High-impact activities

These activities require the appropriate attitude: self-belief, courage and core strength. The tendency is to be too fearful to put yourself out there from fear that the rejection will somehow be final, and that your self-worth is somehow at risk.

o *Write a letter to a casting director*
   In the low-impact activities you will have looked up the name and contact details of a casting director whose work you admire. In the mid-impact activities you will have revised your CV and possibly had new headshots taken. Now is the time to write to a casting director, and ask for a meeting for something that they will be casting in the near future. (See Appendix B for more information.)

o *Make a phone call*
   There will be one phone call that you have been putting off – to your agent, to a casting director, or to a producer. Now is the time to make it.

o *Ask for a 'general'*
   General meetings with casting directors can lead to casting sessions and then on to employment. Write to or email a casting director and ask for a general meeting. Make sure that you come across as warm, professional and employable.

o *Book some rehearsal space*
   Stop waiting for it to happen, and make something happen. Gather together a group of actors, and find a play that you would like to work on, or a story that you would like to tell, and spend some time putting it together. If you share the cost of the rehearsal space, it can work out quite inexpensive,

and this is a small price to pay for feeling creative and honing your skills.

o   *Approach a director you would like to work with*
Let a director know how much you admire their work. Do this by writing an email or a letter, or even going up to them in person. I know an actor who is always seen by a very well-established director when she is casting. He has yet to work with her, but he has been seen by her several times, because he makes a point of keeping in contact.

o   *Set up a meeting with your agent*
Perhaps it is time to talk to your agent about the direction you are going in. Bearing in mind that your agent will have many other actors on their books, it is not a good idea to do this too often. However, now and again, perhaps it is not such a bad idea.

o   *Book a theatre during its down-time*
There is no reason why you should not put on your own production. Small theatres often have a few days or a week free in which nothing is booked, and they might be willing to let you have it under quite favourable terms. Put all your effort into making the play as convincing and sincere as possible. Do not waste time and energy on publicity or inviting hundreds of agents – this will stop you from focusing on the task at hand – but embrace the possibility of sharing your work with your friends and acquaintances.

It is always important that you know why you are doing a job. Unfortunately, productivity does not always equal financial remuneration. Ideally, the reason for doing a potential job will be for both the pay cheque and the creative challenge. However, if there is no fee for a job, have a clear idea of your reasons for being in the play or short film. If you in any way feel exploited or that someone else is benefiting from your efforts, then do not do the job. Think of every piece of work that you do as an investment. Your time is one of your most valuable resources, and by working for nothing you are making a significant invest-ment in the project. Here are some positive reasons for doing a job:

o   A new creative challenge.

o   To gather material for your showreel.

o   The director is someone you have worked with
    before, and you enjoy working with them.

o   It is not your usual casting, and by doing it you will
    get to explore a different type of role.

o   They are an amazing cast from whom you will learn
    a great deal.

o   It will be fun.

Knowing these reasons will empower you and help you to do your best work, and get the most out of the project. Once you have decided what your reasons are, commit fully to the project, and steer clear of conversations about pay or conditions, or any of those topics which actors habitually discuss amongst themselves and which keep them downward-spiralling into inactivity.

The following are not satisfactory reasons to do an unpaid project:

o   You will get seen by a casting director or agent.

o   It may transfer to a larger theatre.

o   The director will probably be famous one day.

o   The playwright will probably be famous one day.

o   Someone involved with the cast or crew has a famous sister/cousin/uncle.

While some of these factors may well be true, they will mostly result in disappointment, and they are not reasons that will sustain you for several weeks' work. The chances are that you will get to the end of the run and experience disappointment that the promise has not been fulfilled. Therefore potential for bitterness is great, because your love of the work was not your main reason for getting involved. Ultimately, it is your love of the work you do which will sustain you and keep you feeling satisfied.

Summary

In this chapter, there are many ideas for keeping yourself productive, both psychologically and practically. Various activities or exercises will help you to take positive and sensible action with regard to enhancing your career. Work out which ones and what sort of balance suits you to keep you at your best, pull you out of the doldrums, and revitalise you after a hectic time. Monitor your state of mind, and reflect on which activities can help you build up momentum so that you remain active, connected and contented.

On the Threshold 5

Auditions, meetings and presentations

For several years, there was some confusion when actors said they were going for 'meetings'. We imagined them having a cosy chat or some sort of interview. Now it is accepted that the word 'meeting' is synonymous with 'audition'. The reason that auditions are now known as meetings in the UK and US is probably a practical one: perhaps the word 'meeting' is less terrifying. It suggests that a dialogue takes place, rather than someone being judged. This is something to bear in mind. Wouldn't you perform better in a 'meeting', rather than in an 'audition'?

We all have our favourite stories about auditions: the young actor so keen to do something different that, while reading the part, she massaged the director's feet; the young actor who was harshly critical about a play he had seen, which turned out to have been directed by the person who was auditioning him; and perhaps most commonly, the actor who simply froze – who couldn't speak, breathe or react.

Meetings are something that all actors have to endure. Only the most successful are cast without first meeting the casting director and director. Even those quite high up the acting food chain are expected to attend a meeting.

All relationships, shallow and deep alike, begin with chance encounters.

David Mitchell (author of *Cloud Atlas* and *The Thousand Autumns of Jacob de Zoet*)

People think that I don't have to audition. Well, I do. I go to meetings like everybody else. The only difference is that I love it. I love going into the room and meeting new people.

Gemma Arterton

Andrew: I know a young actor who went to over fifty auditions before getting her first paid job. She remained hopeful, professional and dignified at all times: slightly amused that she was getting so many meetings, but so little work. In fact, I learned a highly effective trick from this particular actor: keep a 'meetings book' or casting diary.

Exercise: Casting diary

Keep an exercise book for this task. After every meeting, write a record of the date, the role, the production, the name of the production company, the name of the casting director, the name of the director, and a record of who else was at the meeting. Write about what seemed to go well, and what seemed to go badly. Also, make a record of any interesting or quirky conversations that you had. Finally, make a record of how successful you felt it was and then what the outcome was.

After a while you will have a good knowledge of who casts for whom, what sort of parts you are being seen for, and how many times you have been seen by certain production companies. By mentioning in passing some of the information you have recorded, in a second meeting with someone, you can begin to build a professional relationship with directors and casting directors. It is naturally flattering when someone remembers a detail about you, and the impression it makes is great. If you have made a note of what you talked about on a previous occasion; for instance, another play the director had just worked on, making a follow-up enquiry can make the often anonymous process of meetings seem more personal.

The make–or–break moment of meetings occurs on the threshold of the room. How you walk into the room is a pivotal moment which often encapsulates either rejection or acceptance. Bearing in mind that over fifty per cent of all communication is non–verbal, and people who work in casting are experts at reading people, you can assume that these non-verbal attributes radiate from you clearly from the very first moment. There are some qualities which immediately limit any chances that you have of making a positive impression. These are the qualities to be wary of:

o   Desperation

o   Arrogance

o   Overfamiliarity

o   Lethargy

o   Underconfidence

o   Detachment

o   Overt flirtatiousness

This is potentially quite a perplexing list. As you can see, the items on this list can be paired up in opposites: desperation/lethargy; arrogance/underconfidence; overfamiliarity/detachment. They can be summed up as either being too much or too little. This is the fine line that you tread when you are meeting someone for the first time, and the old adage is true: 'The problem with first impressions is that you don't get a second chance.'

These qualities are all physical, and this is what is being read by the casting director:

o   Too much swagger when you walk in.

o   A tense smile.

o   Shoulders hunched.

o   Avoiding eye-contact.

o   A handshake offered too soon.

o   Not standing to your full height.

o   Making your shoulders narrower.

These are all signs that are signalling loud and clear that you are unsuitable for this job, or indeed any job.

Exercise: Impact

Think about someone you know who always makes a positive first impression: the sort of person who is effortlessly likeable. Write down some adjectives that describe this person. Don't move on until you have done this. Actually write the list down, don't just do it in your head.

Perhaps your list included some of the following qualities: open, cheerful, approachable, easy-going, down to earth, matter-of-fact, positive, reliable, relaxed.

It is important that as you go into a meeting, you concentrate on these qualities. Focus on what makes someone likeable, and keep these in mind rather than the previous list – the list of things to avoid being. As you bear these qualities in mind, think to yourself: 'I am open' or 'I am approachable and positive'. Reflect on the physical difference that it is having on you: you are breathing more deeply, you feel broader across the shoulders, you are more released in the neck.

We suggest a mantra or catchphrase to help. As you are waiting to go in to the meeting, simply say to yourself: 'I am really looking forward to meeting these people and getting to know them.' This will immediately improve the way you walk in, and the quality of that all-important first impression.

A word about toes

When you are in a stressful situation, you will often clench your toes. Keep an eye on this before a meeting and during a meeting. If you focus on lengthening your toes, and letting your feet fill your shoes, you will relax into your whole body, breathing in a deeper and more controlled way. In turn this will make you appear more focused, relaxed and in control. You will become someone who people find it easy to spend time with, as your nervousness is not apparent. This is true of hands too, and clenched or fidgety hands are much more visible signs to others.

Part of the issue with meetings might be that you do not consider yourself to be 'on a level' with the person on the other side of the table. As soon as you appear to be needy or even slightly subservient, your professionalism is in jeopardy, and it is a consummate professional attitude that will win the day.

Exercise: Turning the tables

There is a good chance that you are going into meetings thinking 'What can I get from them?', and you look for approval, affirmation or support. If this is the case then you are immediately establishing a parent-child contract. You are taking the role of the child, and you are looking to the casting director as a parent or authority figure. A change of approach is needed: rather than thinking 'What can I get?', think 'What can I offer?' Before the meeting, make a list of what you can offer. Don't move on until you have done this. Actually write the list down, don't just do it in your head:

- Suitability for the part

- Professionalism

- Tenacity

- Openness and a willing attitude

Consider these qualities before you go into the meeting, feel your toes lengthen, your breathing change rhythm, and your body relax. Be aware that you are establishing a very different psychological contract with the director and casting director. 'Psychological contract' is a concept used in business and management training. It is used to define the understanding and expectations that employer and employee have of one another. This then sets the dynamic of the relationship. Once a psychological contract has been subconsciously defined, its parameters become quite set. This makes it even more important that at the point of initial contact, you do not appear to be someone who is seeking approval, and trying to operate within a parent-child transaction.

Under this new psychological contract of two adults who are 'on a level', the result is not personal. You are expressing what you have to offer, and then exploring the suitability and compatibility of this. There is no moral judgement involved: no one has seen your flaws or reasons to dislike you. It is simply a meeting of professional adults. There is little point in getting cross if it does not work out. Don't think of it as a parent (them) punishing or rejecting a child (you). There will be other meetings, and hopefully this adult attitude means that you will have left the meeting having made a good impression. Two professionals have met and explored the possibility of working together on a specific project. This highlights a difference between successful professionals and aspiring unsuccessful actors. The 'adult' actor walks away from the meeting and then gets on with their life, confident in the belief that this was one audition among many, and that equally desirable opportunities will soon arise. The actor with the immature attitude needs to deconstruct the meeting, worry about tiny details, and then spill out their neuroses to their friends. This is unhelpful. You can be sure the casting director will not be indulging in highly strung post-mortems, so we suggest that you too let it go, and move on.

Most casting directors work incredibly hard, and have to do so under extreme time pressure. They are highly skilled at getting the best from actors in auditions, mediating with directors and working around different people's schedules. There are two things to bear in mind when you go into a meeting:

o   They are on your side and are willing you to do well. They want to cast the part after all, and ideally they would like to cast it quickly.

o   They are not to blame if you do not do well; complaining to your agent will only reflect badly on you.

Some tips to help the meeting go more smoothly:

o   Be early. If they want you to do a scene that differs from the one they asked you to look at in advance, you still have time to prepare.

o   Do not cancel or try to reschedule at the last minute. This is inexcusable and you will have no second chance.

o   Learn the 'sides' or pages of the script you have been sent. There is no longer any excuse for not doing this. British actors have to learn from American actors in this respect. An American actor would not dream of reading the script in a meeting, and often American actors will learn as many as ten sides for a meeting. This has now become equally true of theatre auditions as well as television and film. There is no harm in learning the scene that you have been asked to read, and you can guarantee that if you are off-book, the audition will be more creative, more fluid and more impressive. Also, if you have gone to the trouble of learning the part for the audition, your

Casting is ninety-eight per cent of the process, so they want to get it right, and it is important that you are prepared.

Sydney Pollack

61

professionalism will be assured. There will be no anxieties about how reliable you are, as you will have already proven your commitment to the project.

o   Do not express an interest in any part other than the one you are up for. Asking if you can read for another part undermines the skill of the casting director. It shows a lack of commitment to the part that you have been asked to read for. It's also a good idea to read the whole play if it's published, even if you haven't been sent it.

o   If you have been sent the whole script, make sure you have read it and can express your appreciation for it. An excuse like 'Actually I haven't had time to read it' will probably lose you the part. Simple praise for the script is enough: 'I found it really exciting and remained gripped.' You are not expected to give a full academic analysis.

o   Be yourself. There is no right or wrong answer, so do not try to second-guess the director or the casting director by giving a performance you think they want to see but which is not true to you.

Preparation and punctuality are essential. If you are not on time, not off-book with the script, or if you have not bothered to read the whole script so that you can say how much you enjoyed it, then it is your loss. There are plenty of actors who have a more serious and thorough approach, and they will be the ones who get the work. It is not enough to rely on your charm. When so much is at risk, producers will not want to take the chance that this charming, but roguish or scatty actor will be able to do the job. If you were spending hundreds of thousands of pounds a day keeping a production going, would you take a chance on someone who appears unreliable?

Apart from talent and preparation, the casting director and the director are looking for four things:

o   Charisma

o   Openness

o   Bankability

o   Confidence

Let us deal with each separately.

Charisma

Charisma is hard to define, and if we had exercises to develop it, I suspect that we would be millionaires. Charm, charisma, and the ability to be easy-going are elusive qualities.

Exercise: A charismatic attitude

During a conversation with someone, try to be genuinely interested in everything about them: where they have come from; what they have done today; what they are wearing; and what they are saying. Contribute to what they are saying, and make it all about them. Throughout the conversation maintain as much eye contact as feels natural. See if you get a different response from the response that you usually get. Does the person seem more relaxed and open towards you?

This may be one element of charisma: the ability to make the other person feel listened to and attended to. However, it is then equally important to contribute something about yourself. If you have only been 'in attendance' to the other person then the meeting will not have an equal exchange and the other person may feel perplexed or suspicious.

Andrew: It is a well-known prejudice we have about actors that they like to talk exclusively about themselves. This often makes them the figures of ridicule, and to some degree it is true. I know many actors who contact me only when they need something; I help them, of course, but sometimes with a degree of reluctance. One actor I know has a completely different approach. We often go for a cup of tea to discuss a play before he has an audition, and he often phones me before he has a difficult professional decision to make, and I do not mind. I am happy to help. He uses a simple technique. At the beginning of any conversation, he asks me about myself, my family, plays I have seen recently, or work that I am doing. He insists on a few minutes talking about me, before the subject moves on to him, and this can take a substantially longer time. I simply do not mind. He has created the psychological contract between us: we are having a dialogue and he is as interested in me as I am in him. It works. I look forward to hearing from him, and I am always happy to help. I feel that I am investing in this friendship, and not just in his career.

Another element of charisma involves authenticity. Authenticity is viewed as a highly attractive quality; it brings with it sincerity, openness and trust. It implies that nothing is hidden, and you are fearless in being the person you really are. This means, then, that you must have the courage to reveal yourself. We touched on this when we addressed not second-guessing at meetings. You must feel confident that your point of view is worth hearing. What topics of conversation make you become animated, and put a spark in your eye? This is the person that the casting director wants to get to know. What piece of theatre has ignited your enthusiasm? Which performers excite you? Which writers mean something to you? What do you do in your free time that fills you with passion? This is a skill: being able to express an opinion and reveal yourself in a way that is non-threatening, easy-going and non-confrontational.

The casting director Emma Style says that when casting she is looking for someone who would be the perfect host at a cocktail party. This is the degree of charm that Emma expects: warmth, generosity, confidence and grace.

With this in mind, steer clear of controversy in meetings. Never bitch about something you didn't like, or a performer who you think is talentless, or a rumour that you have heard. When you do this, you are downward-spiralling, and your integrity is compromised. When someone is bitchy or indiscreet, everyone in the room asks themselves the same question: 'If they are so willing to be so negative about X, what do they say about *me* behind my back?' You are left without integrity and your charm dissipates into thin air.

There is a theory that casting directors are not actually looking for talent. They are looking for people that everyone can work with.

The charismatic and charming person enables others, is full of belief and keeps possibility open.

Openness

This leads us on to 'openness' as a quality. One characteristic that casting directors are looking for in meetings is that you are not going to be 'trouble'; that you are not going to waste time being argumentative, sulky or diffident. They need reassurance that your creativity is collaborative, and that you are always willing to pick up on a suggestion and embrace its possibility. Here are some other qualities that mean the same as openness: agreeability, approachability, receptiveness, understanding, compliance, cooperation or adaptability.

It is important that you can examine the limits of your own complicity, when exploring how open you are. At what point do you stop collaborating and become obstructive by asserting your own ego? Is it when you feel threatened, or compromised, or morally challenged?

To be honest, we are all as talented as each other. It's whether you fit. Sometimes it boils down to having the right hair.

Maxine Peake

Andrew: I once got a phone call from an actor I had taught. He had been cast in The Tempest, *and was having a disagreement with the director about the type of person Ferdinand is. The director saw him as a typical romantic lead; the actor saw him as a somewhat dishonourable man who had already broken off several engagements. I agreed with the actor. This is the reading of Ferdinand that Shakespeare's text supports. He had already suggested it to the director and it had been dismissed outright. What was he to do next?*

He was a young actor and this was only his third paid job. Was this the point to assert his ego and become less collaborative? Our conversation went as follows:

'Do you enjoy working with this company?'

'Yes.'

'Do you want to work with them again?'

'Yes.'

'Then let go of your interpretation of Ferdinand, and do what the director asks.'

'But the director is wrong.'

'Yes, you know that, and I know that, but it is not worth putting the collaborative process in jeopardy. Just do what the director asks, at most with the tiniest hint of your interpretation, but do what the director asks.'

If this difference in perspective had come up in the audition, and the actor had been less than open, or less than yielding about the director's 'incorrect' interpretation, then he never would have got the job.

This is one of the functions of the meeting: to find out at what point an actor stops being collaborative and cooperative; to find out when, if ever, the actor stops being open.

Bankability

Let us turn our attention to our third element: 'bankability'. If you end up being cast in a part, you are contributing to someone's investment. Money, time, effort and attention are all being invested in a project, and you must show that you are not going to undermine this investment. Even a fringe play costs several thousand pounds to rehearse, market and stage, so a film, a piece of television or a theatre tour costs many thousands or hundreds of thousands. In the meeting, one of your jobs is to demonstrate that you are worthy of this investment.

Exercise: Your bankability

Reflect on the following two questions:

- Look at the CV you are presenting to casting directors. What is on the CV that shows you are bankable?

- If there is nothing on the CV, how are you going to reassure them in the meeting?

It should come as no surprise, then, that both Freema Agyeman and Karen Gillan had small parts in *Doctor Who* before taking the much-coveted roles of the Doctor's companion. They had proved to the producers that they were reliable, professional and talented, and that it was worth taking a risk on them because they were bankable. Perhaps you now begin to understand why getting work as an actor is such a slow process: you have to build your house brick by brick, as you show to your future employers that you are worth their backing.

It is possible for an actor to prove themselves as bankable even if they do not have an impressive CV. This is done at the meeting by exuding steadfast confidence. A confident actor who has just graduated can appear just as bankable as a seasoned professional, if they exude the right attitude. In fact, it is possible that a newly graduated actor will appear even more bankable, as they have something very exciting to offer: their newness. Every casting director or director wishes to discover a fresh new talent. However, this actor must be able to instil confidence in his or her future employer.

Confidence

Many young actors seem to see 'confidence' as a dirty word. However, as this chapter began with the idea of a successful actor treading a thin line between two extremes in meetings, let us address the notion of confidence. Confidence is not somehow akin to arrogance. This is only the case when the actor does not really believe in themselves, and they somehow overcompensate. Confidence is a highly attractive quality; arrogance is not. Confidence makes everyone feel at ease; arrogance simply irritates. Confidence is the sign of a professional; arrogance is a sign of the aspiring amateur. What then is the distinction?

Confidence is a quality which is full of ease and lightness of touch. It is the expression of a clear belief in ability. Confidence signals 'I can do this job; I believe that I am the best person for it – so trust me.' Arrogance has a weight and striving behind it. It is full of effort. The arrogant actor tries to convince the casting director as they try to convince themselves. It is a product of self-doubt, and it makes everyone around feel ill at ease and reluctant to engage. An actor who truly believes that they can do the job – and is aware of what they have to offer – need never worry about being perceived as arrogant. In fact, as acting requires nerves of steel, and an incomparable fearlessness, confidence is a highly bankable quality.

It is a good idea when you go to a meeting to look the part. This need not mean a full method-acting approach: going unwashed and scruffy if you are auditioning for the part of a tramp; or looking sexually available if you are going for the part of a seductress. But a suggestion of the part that you are about to play will certainly help along the director's imagination. Wear a suit if the part is mainly set in a business environment, or smart-casual if the part demands it. If it is a period piece, then by all means suggest it in something you wear, or something you do with your hair. If you go for an out-and-out period look, you will simply alienate everyone. Caution is to be recommended with regard to exposing flesh. This is true for men with unbuttoned shirts and shorts as much as for women with short skirts and cleavage. Your professionalism must not be compromised on any account. It is fine to suggest a certain air of sensuality, but the casting director or director must also feel comfortable and safe with you at all times. This will not be the case if they are spending the time worrying about a part of your body popping out rather than focusing on your talent and your personality.

It is inevitable that you will make a mess of a meeting at some point in your career; you may say something foolish, or simply have an 'off day' and appear unresponsive. On these occasions, the best thing to do is simply to take responsibility that it was your mistake, learn from it, then let it go and put it down to experience. I have known actors go to extraordinary lengths when they have messed up: they write emails explaining that they have suffered a recent bereavement; they invite the casting director out to lunch by way of apology; they send grovelling cards. None of these are effective – they simply undermine your professionalism, and, frankly, the casting director will not be all that bothered. They are (mostly) human beings who understand that you are also fallible and entitled to have a bad day.

Actors often forget that meetings are two-way transactions. As well as assessing you, it is an opportunity for *you* to meet *them*, and decide whether *you* would like to work with *them*. This is a very important shift in focus. If a young, ambitious director's conceptualised production of *Macbeth* is distasteful to you, then it is probably better that you have met him in advance before you invest six weeks of your life suffering under his tyranny. Bear in mind that this investigation of compatibility is a mutual process and this will help you to keep the meeting on a level, operating on the basis of adult transactions. Remembering this will help to calm down any feelings of desperation and will help to make you appear professional and in control. So, when you go into a meeting, ask:

o   'What can I offer?', rather than 'What can I get from them?'

o   Is our way of working compatible?' rather than 'Will they like me?'

While it is useful to have a classical speech up your sleeve, it is unlikely that you will be asked to perform one in auditions. You may perhaps be asked to prepare one for an audition for a Shakespeare play, but it is likely that this will be the only occasion. For most auditions you will be told which scene to prepare, or sent some sides in advance. On occasion you may be asked to sight-read. There are a few things to bear in mind when sight-reading:

o   If you are a poor reader or you experience dyslexia, it is imperative that you let the casting director know in advance so that you can be given enough time to prepare.

o   You must 'own' the text, and make it look like you are really speaking it, rather than reading it in a 'storytelling for six-year-olds' way.

o   The *information* in the script is more important than the *emotion*. We generally do not like spending time with people who try to make us feel something. We call these people overbearing, hysterical or histrionic. Keeping the information more apparent than the feeling will help to make your sight-reading appear more authentic and real.

o   When you read, stress the noun with the adjective: '*greedy pig*' rather than '*greedy* pig'; and the verb with the adverb: 'She was *eating ravenously*' rather than 'She was eating *ravenously*.' This helps to make it sound less 'acted'.

o   Poor acting is excusable; dull and underenergised acting is never forgiven.

One final tip for auditions: crying is easy, any actor can do it, and it makes everyone feel slightly uncomfortable. It is much more effective in a scene – if the circumstances require it – to make it look like you are trying to stop yourself crying. Ironically this makes you appear like a much more emotionally available actor than an actor who can simply sob convincingly.

Summary

Remember that meetings offer an opportunity for mutual dialogue; you are meeting them and they are meeting you. Try to be 'on a level' in the meeting, rather than appearing inferior or superior, and keep any desperation out of the room. Prepare thoroughly and do not rely on inherent charm. Look the part, be professional and show that you are worth investing in.

An Actor Like No Other 6

Know yourself

This is one of the most paradoxical and potentially frustrating areas when you are working as an actor. It is paradoxical because in your mind you might be perfect for a part, but directors, casting directors and producers might have a completely different idea of who you are and what you represent. It can be frustrating because this is one of the areas of your life that you have least control over. You are therefore mostly dependent on what others think and the decisions that they make. However, there is still something that can be done. By exploring your casting potential thoroughly, you may be able to be more prepared for what to expect. There is no guarantee that this will make you more successful or happier, but it may ease some of the disappointment, help you focus on your key strengths, and also open up new possibilities of the casting you are suitable for.

Casting in film, television and theatre all have a slightly different approach. You may well find that the process in film and television is more pedestrian and less creative. In film and television, you may well only get cast according to type, and the process may be quite laborious, involving many meetings and callbacks. You may have to wait between meetings as the feedback from different producers can take some time. The range of characters you are cast as may be quite narrow, and once you are known for acting one thing on screen, this may be what you are cast as

For I must tell you friendly in your ear, sell when you can: you are not for all markets.

As You Like It,
Act III, Scene v

again and again. This has as much to do with audience expectation as it does with the caution of producers. Audiences want to know what they are getting, and producers want to know what they are paying for. Working in theatre may give you greater opportunities to explore a more diverse range of characters, and perhaps even show that you are capable of portraying something radically different. As crude as it may seem, this general rule is true: the more money something costs to produce, the more cautious the producers are going to be about taking risks. There are, of course, exceptions to this, and a more adventurous and creative approach to casting is to be welcomed by actors.

Most actors acknowledge the mystery of the casting process, and some also understand the parameters of their casting, and know to what degree they can push the boundaries. These actors might be reluctant to waste their energy pursuing roles for which they are clearly not suitable, and worrying about why they have not been cast. Every actor fits into an immediate and obvious type and, regardless of how flexible you might be within the boundaries of this, it is essential that you understand what your type is in terms of *playing age*, *demographic* and *typical character*. You may have the opportunity to explore characters outside these parameters, but it is more likely that you remain cast as your type again and again throughout your career. For example, there might be a very good chance that you will never get to play an action hero or a romantic lead within mainstream commercial theatre or film. Once you have understood your casting you will have a much better idea of what it is that you are selling. This will help you to become more focused in understanding what you do well and how to put this to use. You can take comfort from the fact that as you grow older and change, so does your casting. However, at any stage, you are vulnerable to how you are perceived, and the nature of your type.

Usually, casting is based around type. Having a good grasp of what type you appear to be can be useful. Drama schools may train actors to be chameleons and develop versatility, but this is not what is always required in the real world. Producers and casting directors often demand an immediacy in what type you represent. Often the best policy is to think about how you appear to be, and who you are best able to portray. This advice is most applicable to television and film. As we have already discussed, within casting for theatre, there tends to be a greater degree of flexibility.

Let us consider one such example of this: *Another Country*. This was a successful play by Julian Mitchell, which was made into a film in 1984. The play was based on the school days of the spy Guy Burgess, and set in a British public school in the 1930s. The two main characters in the film were played by Rupert Everett and Colin Firth (who had also both appeared on stage). If we examine the careers of both of these actors over the last twenty-five years, it becomes clear that neither has strayed too far away from their original class demographic. Whether Mr Darcy in *Pride and Prejudice*, Lord Wotton in *Dorian Gray*, or King George VI in *The King's Speech*, Colin Firth's casting has remained consistent: upper-middle-class or upper-class, gentlemanly and cultured. He also seems to be cast as characters who are slightly melancholic or in some way looking for happiness or love. Rupert Everett's career has continued along similar lines; often playing upper-middle-class or upper-class characters. He has developed a specialism for playing characters who are sarcastic, witty and iconoclastic. In 2002, Firth and Everett were reunited in the film version of *The Importance of Being Earnest*, each playing to their expected strengths: Rupert Everett playing the more deceitful and foppish Algernon; Colin Firth the more innocent Jack.

There is an irony at work here: as people, neither Colin Firth nor Rupert Everett are necessarily the type that they portray consistently. Colin Firth did not grow up as one of the privileged upper class. His parents were both teachers and he went to a normal British comprehensive school. There is an important lesson to learn. How you appear is not necessarily representative of who you really are.

Knowing how you are perceived is essential. It is important that you reflect on your type, and how you come across. It would appear that your type is almost predetermined. For example, are you a romantic lead or a cheeky best friend? Are you seen as a sexual predator or an ingénue? Are you naturally authoritative or subservient? It is astonishing how often we meet actors in our workshops who have little or no idea of what their casting is.

Here is an exercise to do with a group of friends whom you trust to be honest with you. The results can be quite shocking, so brace yourself.

Exercise: *Romeo and Juliet*

This is not an exercise about casting in Shakespeare. We are simply using *Romeo and Juliet* as an example because the archetypes in the play are so distinct. This exercise will help you to view yourself as others view you. It will help you to narrow down how suitable you are for various roles. *Romeo and Juliet* is the vehicle that we use. Actually, you can repeat this exercise using all sorts of different films and plays – all that is needed is a range of different men, or a range of different women. Do not consider age as a factor in this exercise, so remove all age restrictions. We simply wish to concentrate on type.

If you are a woman, consider the following roles:

● Juliet

● The Nurse

● Lady Capulet

If you are a man, consider the following:

- Romeo
- Benvolio
- Mercutio

Which would you be asked to play, regardless of age? Which is your type? Each type is clearly distinct. An actor who is suitable for Romeo would not be asked to play Benvolio or Mercutio. The same is true for the women. The Nurse is clearly a different type from either Juliet or Lady Capulet. There is rarely any confusion in this matter. You would only ever be considered for one role. Let us look at this in more detail. Here are some adjectives to describe each character:

Juliet: innocent, intelligent, discerning, loyal, individual, courageous

Nurse: extrovert, bawdy, extravagant, playful, expedient, aware, subservient

Lady Capulet: dignified, authoritative, maternal, detached, sensual

And for the men:

Romeo: romantic, good-looking, idealistic, needy, boyish, vulnerable, open, innocent

Benvolio: solid, dependable, sympathetic, pragmatic, loyal

Mercutio: extrovert, witty, comedic, irreverent, individual, scathing, impetuous, bawdy

When you look at these adjectives, you can see how mutually exclusive each part is. An actor who would be cast as Lady Capulet would simply never be asked to play the Nurse.

In our workshops, we have found how unaware some actors are of their type. Often, an actor considers themselves suitable for one type, but everyone else sees them as something else. Discovering which type you are can often be a sudden shock – a confusing and overwhelming discovery. Adjusting can take time. In one of our workshops, a young woman refused to see herself as someone who might play Juliet. The entire group unanimously cast her as Juliet, though. She appeared innocent, gentle, intelligent and youthful, but this was not how she was willing to present herself to the world; she considered herself to be a Nurse-type – bawdy, brash and extrovert. The participants in the workshop perceived someone sensitive, demure, modest and attractive. Little wonder, then, that with this lack of self-knowledge, she was going to auditions and not getting cast in the roles she wanted.

Before you can consider going to meetings and auditions, it is essential that you are aware of how others see you, and the only way to do this is to get feedback. Ultimately, this knowledge is empowering and enabling, despite the potential initial shock. Knowing what type you appear to be will give you the opportunity to moderate how you come across. If your natural type fulfils the specifics of the role, then you will know that you are playing to your strengths. However, if the role falls outside the parameters of how you are perceived, then you will have to make a special effort to come across in a specific way, which will be different from the way in which you normally operate.

This chapter is not meant to discourage your creativity, nor do we want to limit possibility. However, this type of self-knowledge is essential for an actor. Casting is not always as creative as we would like it to be, but it is important to understand that the financial investment is often huge, and production companies understandably want to exercise caution and minimise the risks.

Always be a first-rate version of yourself, instead of a second-rate version of somebody else.

Judy Garland

When Shakespeare's plays are being cast, the types are as distinct as in the *Romeo and Juliet* exercise. Shakespeare was writing for a world with an inflexible hierarchy, and he was writing for a company of actors in which he had specific types: for example, aristocrat, tyrant, rebel, young lover, vagabond, comic servant, loyal courtier, trusted advisor. It is unlikely that an actor suitable for Falstaff would be suitable to play Richard II.

Exercise: Shakespeare's worlds

In Shakespeare's plays, several worlds converge. For example, *Much Ado About Nothing* involves the soldiers; Leonato's court; the constables. *The Tempest* involves the courtiers from Naples; those who live on the island; the servants from the ship. Pick a play and think about the worlds that the play involves. Ask yourself the following questions:

● Which world would I be most suited to if I was cast in the play?

● What physical attributes make me most suited to this casting?

● What behavioural qualities make me most suited to this casting?

● How would I approach being cast in a different world in the same play?

Do this for several plays, and then compare notes with someone else who has done the exercise.

It is also important to know which ethnicity you are considered to be. It often comes as a surprise to actors to discover that they would quite easily pass for Mediterranean or Middle Eastern. Again, this is not a statement on who you are, but it is important to know how you are perceived.

Fortunately, we are moving into a time where, for theatre, ethnicity matters less than acting ability: black actors Adrian Lester and David Oyelowo have played Shakespeare's Henry V (at the National Theatre) and Henry VI (for the RSC), respectively. Film and television are less flexible. The purpose of this book is not to discuss the degree of stereotyping in film and television casting, so we will proceed without further comment. However, it is perhaps useful to know that in the UK there is a shortage of Asian actors and also a shortage of middle-aged African-Caribbean actors.

In terms of casting and ethnicity, this is a personal matter. It is important that you do not feel that your integrity has been compromised in how you have been cast. If you think that you are being exploited by portraying a particular role, then it is best to turn it down.

What about other elements of casting: are you a leading actor or a character actor, and what is the distinction? The difference between a lead and a character is how you come across; if you are quirky, unusual or eccentric – even if you are very good-looking – then you are probably a character actor. There is little point in complaining about the injustice of it all, or about the superficial judgements that are made about people. Perhaps the term 'character actor' is a polite way of saying 'not typically attractive'. This is no bad thing. Think of the number of character actors who have had remarkable careers: Jon Lovitz, Roger Lloyd Pack, Julie Walters, Lisa Kudrow, to name a few. It is also comforting to reflect on the fact that most actors become character actors as they grow older.

Exercise: Character or lead?

It is important to know how you do come across. Write down three adjectives that you imagine spring to mind when people think about you.

If you are a lead actor, these might be:

Strong, determined, motivated, principled, energetic, enthusiastic, calm, responsible, regular, conformist, sexy, attractive, athletic, sporty, daring

If you are a character actor, then your list might include:

Quirky, neurotic, flaky, absent-minded, down-trodden, marginalised, jovial, flippant, anarchic, non-conformist, foolhardy, androgynous, confused

It is possible that you are finding this discussion a little disheartening or dispiriting – you do not want to see yourself as someone who fits a ready-made mould. This is not actually the case, and thinking in this way becomes reductive and limiting. You are, of course, unique. You have something to offer that nobody else can, and it is important to spend some time reflecting on this.

I was lucky not to have been born pretty.

Joan Hickson

You are beginning to think about what you have to offer and how you might fit in to other people's perception. It is now time to address what makes you special as an actor; it is time to think about your USP: your *Unique Selling Point*. What is it about you that sets you apart from all other actors? Which roles could you go and audition for with the utmost confidence that you are the right person for the role? Try the following exercise.

Exercise: One hundred actors in the room

This imaginative exercise will help you to locate your Unique Selling Point. If there were a hundred actors of your gender and age in a room, and a casting director started trying to narrow down the number according to the criteria required, which attributes would get you down to the final two or three? For example, if they were to state that only actors who would convincingly pass as businessmen were required, how many people would leave the room? Now they are looking for people who appear down-trodden or defeated. Suddenly there are only twenty people in the room. Of these, they want quirky, comedic characters. You are in the final five. How could you refine the process further? Which criteria would get you into the final few or even be the final one?

DIRECTOR. *We are looking for somebody different.*

MICHAEL DORSEY. *I can be different.*

DIRECTOR. *I know. We are looking for somebody else.*

Tootsie, dir. Sydney Pollack, 1982

Once you are aware that you are the right type, you can concentrate on the meeting going smoothly, rather than worrying that you would be unusual casting for this role. Setting your hopes on playing a character who is a thuggish type is a waste of time and energy, unless you fit this type convincingly. It is not your job to change the casting director's mind. The opening sequence of the film *Tootsie* gives an idea of how an actor can appear desperate when he believes he can play anything and everything. Like Dustin Hoffman's character, Michael Dorsey, setting your sights on roles without any sense of discernment can be a futile and exhausting experience.

Having a USP or 'personal brand' is not about narrowing your options unnecessarily. It may be that there are two or three types of roles or characters which you would ideally be able to play. Being mercurial or very flexible in your casting is not part of your USP. This is certainly true at the beginning of your career. Many actors resist this idea, and believe that it is being adaptable which makes them easy to cast. This is fair enough. There is a good chance that they have spent three years at drama school learning how to be adaptable and malleable. However, it is better to concentrate on the concrete qualities you have. This is the key element which makes you bankable. The most important thing is that you know what your USP is and that you market yourself in this way. This may mean having a very clear conversation with your agent about which parts you are going for and, indeed, choosing an agent that is most likely to place you in these potential situations. Other feedback from friends and family, fellow actors and casting directors should be reflected on to consolidate how you see yourself, and are seen, as an actor.

Exercise: The one-liner

Summarise in one sentence, but with clear details, what it is that you do. In a businesslike context, to describe yourself simply as an actor is not enough. Remember the scene in *Notting Hill*: Julia Roberts' character is asked by someone who is unaware of her global fame what she does for a living. With delicious irony she simply replies 'An actor.' For anyone with this degree of success, their USP is obvious and needs no discussion.

Here are some examples of actors and the one-liners we imagine might apply:

Patricia Routledge: I expertly play social-climbing characters who appear to be their own worst enemy.

Richard Wilson: I excel at irritable elderly characters who still have a great deal to learn.

Adrian Brody: My vulnerability is apparent and I play outsiders in a unique and convincing way.

Anne Hathaway: While I appear appealingly normal, potential dangers lurk beneath my charm.

When you have devised your own sentence, practise saying it to as many people as possible, and adjust it accordingly until you feel it is just right. For example, Lucy progressed her one-liner from 'I am an actress' to 'I am at my best playing young, tragic lead roles' through several iterations to 'I excel at portraying troubled characters in extreme situations and my acting is most suited to theatre'. Print or write it out and put it in a place where you see it often. Revisit your one-liner at least every three months to check that it is still in keeping with your vision: the work you want and know you are right for.

Determination comes into play in the moments when you feel most alone. The moments when you must drive yourself to put in the work without encouragement or support. Determination is putting your heart and soul into an audition, only to have it thrown back in your face, being able to forget about it and then do it all over again.

Bradley James

Once your one-liner is rolling off your tongue at meetings, at play readings and other networking events, you will find that opportunities for exactly that kind of work come your way more than ever before. You will have built yourself a reputation as being that sort of actor. Once you have a few more examples of having done the type of work your USP specifies, you will grow in confidence about saying what you do – and begin only going for work that is right for you. This will improve your hit-rate and build your confidence and your personal brand further. Sometimes this can occur in reverse and this is worth examining. This can happen if you have a very strong look that others can spot immediately. If you are not one hundred per cent sure of your direction, but you keep getting certain types of work, it may be worth looking at why this is happening. If you cannot work that out yet, just observe the patterns and accept what they are telling you. If you keep getting cast in period dramas, it may be that your appearance or diction are strongly reminiscent of this era. But regardless of the various reasons that there may be, you would do well to market yourself strongly as this type.

Andrew: I know an actor who is desperate to do gritty kitchen-sink-style drama. However, he gets a great deal of work doing heightened comedy and character comedy. Perhaps he should capitalise on this more, and realise how his talent for comedy is seen as something unique and highly bankable.

Focus on knowing who you are from a practical and technical angle, as well as from a branding and marketing perspective. You will start to build a multilayered picture of yourself in the business of acting. This multilayered perspective will expand as you work through this book. As a successful actor, *you* are your business, and as part of operating as such, you have to understand exactly what it is that you are selling. Most actors are natural extroverts and the notion of selling yourself will eventually come quite naturally. However, this may not be the case for everyone and certainly not all the time. Also, perhaps this is not really a skill that they teach at most drama schools, and it becomes harder the longer you have been out of work. Getting the right agent, steadily building your reputation and experience, and promoting yourself in an authentic and confident way are the basics.

Summary

The Job's in the Bag

The chemistry of nervousness

Lucy, the recent graduate from drama school whom we first met in Chapter 1, eventually sought help from a psychological coach after experiencing panic attacks and stage fright. She said that in the moments leading up to auditioning, she would work herself up into a terrible state owing to overwhelming feelings of self-doubt. Her mouth felt so dry that she feared she would hardly be able to talk; the muscles in her legs became so tight that she thought she would freeze on the spot; she would sweat profusely which made her even more self-conscious and embarrassed; and she ended up clenching her fists to try to 'get a grip'. Sometimes it was so extreme that she even thought she would be sick or wet herself. Feeling desperate, she would sometimes speak or behave inappropriately and regret it later. The more incidents like this that she could recall, the worse it became, to the point that she was making excuses not to go to auditions at all. Finally, her agent suggested that she seek advice from her doctor. After explaining her issue, she was told the story of a rock star (we will call him Mick), well known for his flamboyant performances, who described the moments before a gig as so exciting that he licked his lips, felt the fine layer of perspiration making his skin glow, and embraced the warm feeling in his chest and the burning in his abdomen. With muscles taut, he bounded onto stage, tossed his trademark mane of hair and the rest was history.

Worry affects the circulation, the heart, the glands, the whole nervous system. I have never known a man who died from overwork, but many who died from doubt.

Charles Horace Mayo

Lucy took on board the power of developing a positive mindset and worked successfully with a psychological coach to overcome her anxieties. The exercises and techniques that she used to get back on track are included throughout this book, as well as an explanation of why actors can get to feeling like this, and what can be done to prevent going down this route. Lucy had been experiencing a reality – for her – that was debilitating and fear-inducing, but she also knew the dangers of going down the 'self-medication' route like some of her peers. For example, she had started drinking lots of coffee before auditions to try and perk herself up, but this only made things worse as it dehydrated her further and contributed to her jitters rather than staying calm and reminding herself of her purpose. Looking back, she could see that Mick was experiencing basically an almost identical set of emotional and physical 'symptoms' as her, but interpreting them as a completely different experience – something positive, empowering and inspiring. This provided phenomenal amounts of confidence and energy:

Actual symptoms	Lucy's reaction	Mick's reaction
Dry mouth	Drink coffee or not be able to speak	Lick lips, chew gum or sip water
Tense muscles	Feeling frozen	A signal that he was ready for action
Sweating	Embarrassed	Glowing
Butterflies in stomach	Feeling sick	Excited

After each of the following sections, there will be exercises like the ones that Lucy used to conquer her fears and move from responding as she had been, towards feeling more like Mick. In each category, you should choose a technique that appeals to you or challenge yourself with one you have not tried before. Play around with them all, over time, trying each one for at least a week and taking forward the ones you find most useful, until they become a habit. Remember that forming new thought patterns and habits takes time, so just do something – however small – each day to reach your new way of being; keep believing that it will make a big difference. Reprogramming your thoughts to eradicate behaviour patterns that are barriers to your success is certainly possible with patience and determination and can lead to great rewards. However, there are no short cuts, and the exercises in this chapter will need to be incorporated into your daily routine to achieve this. Remember that you chose to become an actor, and remember why you did. You may experience some difficulties with this at times, but it will be worth it when you attain the success that you have envisaged for yourself.

Emotions

There are eight basic human emotions of which five are fear, anger, disgust, shame and sadness.[1] These are all *survival emotions*, generating various complicated behaviours such as running away, hiding or overeating. One emotion (surprise/ startle) is a *threshold emotion*; it can flip your emotional state between *survival emotions* and one or both of the other main type of emotions, namely *attachment emotions*, such as excitement/joy and love/trust. So, five of the eight primary emotions are to do with survival. That makes it understandable why it is so much easier to create motivation based on fear rather than joy: for example, compare a threat like 'You're not posh enough; you don't have the public-school background, so you won't get

Every single night I'm nervous. You never know how the audience is going to react.

Vivien Leigh

the parts you want' with the excitement and joy of 'You don't have to reinvent yourself; there are plenty of lower-middle-class roles: single mum, policeman's wife, receptionist – you're fine as you are.' The energy that comes from the *survival emotions* like fear or shame goes inwards to protect you from humiliation and rejection by keeping you away from situations in which you might be exposed to these. The energy that comes from the two *attachment emotions* goes outwards into nurture and creativity. With the attention outwards, you are in an effective mode for performance. If you are in a position where you feel that all you can do is fight for your survival, you will not have the emotional energy to generate the excitement that leads to creative thinking and putting yourself up for challenges. The energy that comes from the *threshold emotion* – surprise/startle – is cleverly used by stand-up comedians, the big-dipper industry and horror-film makers, among others. They hold audiences in thrall by the element of surprise until it becomes clear what is going to happen, and therefore whether you should be horrified or delighted.

Survival emotions	Attachment emotions	Threshold emotions
Fear	Excitement / Joy	Surprise / Startle
Anger		
Disgust		
Shame	Love / Trust	
Sadness		

It is popularly thought that the *survival emotions* are 'negative' and the *attachment emotions* are 'positive'. This is not always the case, as they are part of a complex system in which it is possible to experience them all at the same time. This is the reason we sometimes create confusion about how we feel, or feel conflicted inside – do you recognise the combination of being nervous and exhilarated when facing a new challenge? Or feeling pleased to see another actor who is a friend doing well, but feeling envious at the same time? This is what being human is – the ability to have complex emotions and, if we have had the fortune to be well-nurtured, these become the feelings that bring colour and meaning to our lives. By the time you become an adult who has chosen to be an actor, it is possible to take ownership over how you let yourself feel and react to external events. The more you become practised at recognising your emotions, the easier it will be to handle them.

Exercise: Adapting to and managing the various states of being

- Start each day with a positive statement of how well the day will go. This could be something as simple as 'I'll have a great day today!' but try to stretch yourself and make the statement better than what you might expect, or be specific: 'My day will be full of interesting people' or 'Many opportunities will come my way today'.

- Once you have noticed the reactive emotional states you tend to get into, you might notice that these are patterns which occur across the spectrum of your life – in your professional and personal (family, social and romantic) situations and relationships. For example, a tendency to become dejected after a rejection may be reflected in your reaction to not getting a job as

---

well as not making things work with a partner. A tendency to be more resilient usually occurs in many areas in one person's life. Also, you might have been operating in this way for many years, perhaps even since childhood. Simply noticing these patterns may be half the battle won, as 'awareness is curative.'[2] Try reframing them – for example, when you are feeling impatient, think of it as an opportunity to practise positive thinking.

- Develop a catchphrase or mantra to help you cope in stressful situations. Think about yourself in a successful situation. Visualise it and ask yourself what it looks like, what it feels like, what it sounds like. Use your answer to these questions to come up with a mantra. For example, Andrew was imagining directing a film that he has in development, and the mantra that came to him when visualising this was 'I am the culmination of all my work.' Tara makes her mantra (for interviews) – 'They are seriously considering me' – even more powerful by combining it with a simple physical action that reinforces it as she visualises success – she touches the face of her watch.

- Take some deep breaths, try a yoga class or experiment with simple meditation techniques.

- Listen to some 'mood music' (experiment with how different types of music affect your moods). Treat yourself to an aromatherapy bath or a diffuser. Music and smell are strongly linked to the mood centres in your brain through your auditory and olfactory nerves – so this does work.

Anxiety

Sadly, anxiety can become a daily reality for most actors. Anxiety comes about through a branch of the nervous system that mediates the survival emotions. This existed to give primitive man a survival advantage when hunting and gathering in open terrain where they were vulnerable to attack. Through the nervous system and adrenaline from adrenal glands (sitting just above the kidneys), we get the fight and flight reactions that allowed our ancestors to either confront the situation (fight) or escape (flight). These days we are more often confronted with and concerned about psychological threats to our status and independence than actual physical threats, but these are experienced in the same way by our brains. This hypothetical 'attack' has the same effect as a literal attack. What usually happens to us when we perceive that we are under threat – and therefore feel anxious – is that our pupils open wider to let more light into our eyes, the fine hairs on our bodies stand on end (to allow sweating which regulates body temperature), major muscle groups contract so that they are ready for action, our heart beats faster and we breathe more rapidly. The 'butterflies in the stomach' feeling is thought to be caused by the dense input of nerves from the emotional centres of the brain to the gut – more evidence that your 'gut instinct' is there for a purpose, and if you become well attuned to what it is telling you, it could be used to your advantage. Short bursts of adrenaline can actually lead to improved performance, but if it takes over and you cannot exercise mind over matter, then it can actually impair your performance like it did for Lucy. Not dealing healthily with stressful situations can lead to extreme anxiety, panic attacks and chronic stress – all of these naturally make you less creative.

Exercise: Raising awareness of how you are feeling emotionally, mentally and physically

- Keep a diary of events and how you feel during them. Reflect on how you interacted at an audition and write it down, noticing what was going on in your mind, how you behaved, how your body was performing and how people reacted to you. Record how using stimulants like coffee make you feel and behave differently.

- Every hour, or at least four times daily, ask yourself how you are feeling and explore why. For example, 'I am feeling agitated and this could be because I am worried where the next piece of work is going to come from' or 'I am feeling excited because I am meeting up with an old friend from drama school who always makes me feel more positive about myself.' Even if you do not know why you feel a certain way, acknowledge this – it may dawn on you later.

- When you have time to relax every so often, perhaps in the bath or in bed at night, take time to explore the condition of your body. Is your skin dry? Is your hair and scalp in good condition? Are your shoulders tense? Do you have mouth ulcers or a cold sore? Are you going to the loo regularly? Get to know your body and how it works really well and look after it – as an actor, you are your own greatest asset.

Stress

The world of acting, like many other professions, can create stress for those who inhabit it, which in turn can become incredibly demotivating. This is the danger of letting anxiety go on for so long that it becomes an accepted part of your life. Stress:

o   Can affect your thoughts causing poor concentration
      and low self-esteem.

o   Can affect your emotions leading to irritability or
      even anger.

o   Is sometimes followed by changes in behaviour, like
      difficulty falling asleep, mood swings, and even
      physical symptoms such as heartburn, backache or a
      tension headache.

This is because there are several mechanisms whereby how you feel psychologically affects your health; namely, adrenaline, serotonin ('the happy chemical') and cortisol ('the stress hormone'): these are all simply chemical compounds in the nervous and hormonal systems. The problem is that stress is usually psychological, meaning it is caused by perceptions such as loss of control, threats to self-esteem or fear of failure. Stress happens when people feel that the pressures on them are more than they can cope with. This then affects your health. Minor ailments contributed to by stress include frequent colds, flu, indigestion, muscle aches and acne. These may be significant and need to be taken seriously. Experience of stress, if sustained over long periods, can have a powerful and widespread negative impact on health and well-being. Cortisol is released in a sharp burst first thing in the morning to help you get started for the day. It exists at a baseline level in all our systems, but can peak again during the day at times of stress. Having lots of ups and downs of cortisol in your blood can weaken your immune system. Being aware of what goes on in your body when you are stressed, and being able to manage this effectively is an enormously helpful ability for work and life. This applies in any walk of life, but the benefits for actors are clear, not only when you are working on a part but also in your downtime. Ask yourself honestly how familiar this feeling of stress is to you and how much damage it could be doing to you in the long-term.

Perhaps you are experiencing some of these ill-effects already: poor concentration, low self-esteem, anxiety, anger, sleeplessness, irritability, heartburn, tension headaches? The following exercises can help you deal with stress in a way that will suit you.

Exercise: Enjoying the here and now

- Try to live in the present moment rather than holding on to regrets from the past or worries about your future. If thoughts such as regret, bitterness or resentment come in to your mind, practise letting go of them each time you breathe out.

- Take five minutes every morning to reflect quietly – go for a walk and notice the sky or sounds of nature around you; have a cup of tea or herbal tea and really taste it; notice your breathing patterns and any tension in particular parts of your body, and relax while breathing slowly and deeply.

- If a particular issue is bothering you, have a look at the 'change curve' diagram on page 99 and work out if you are stuck in one of the phases and why. Set aside some time to work through the feelings that you are experiencing. Accept them as part of a normal process that all actors go through from time to time. You can develop your resilience by learning from each situation and taking responsibility for dealing with it differently next time. It is easy to get stuck, or shuttle back and forth between two of the stages such as anger and blame, after not getting seen for a part, *if* you don't understand the process of change. But if you do, half the battle is won and you can move from acceptance to responsibility. Conscious strategies are required to recognise and deal with this.

Depression

Depression is mediated by a neurotransmitter called serotonin. In depression, the brain receptors which are sensitive to serotonin become reduced or desensitised to its effects. This leads to chronic low mood and other widespread symptoms. If (constantly for two weeks or more) you have had feelings of hopelessness, helplessness or worthlessness, as well as two or more from the list below, this might be a warning sign that you are suffering from depression.

This is not how other people normally think or feel – it is a dysfunctional state, and you do not have to live like this. You should see your GP to discuss the options, which might include counselling-type therapy and/or medication. Whichever option is chosen, it takes at least two weeks for the brain receptors to return to normal, and with medications you may experience side-effects, so give yourself the time and space necessary to recuperate completely.

Symptoms of depression:

o   Poor sleep (especially waking up early every morning without feeling refreshed).

o   Change of appetite (usually loss), and losing (or gaining) a lot of weight.

o   No energy, even to do things you used to enjoy.

o   Forgetting things and not being able to concentrate on a topic for long.

Exercise: After recovery – unblocking creativity

- Each morning make a list of things that happened the previous day for which you are grateful. Include seemingly random coincidences that worked in your favour.

- Take time in the shower or after doing some exercise to appreciate parts of your body. For the purposes of this chapter, concentrate on your brain, adrenal glands (where adrenaline is produced), skin, guts and immune system. Be thankful for the functions that they perform and how they are helping you towards your goals. This is a great thing to do on the morning of an audition – pamper yourself and appreciate your posture, bright eyes, well-modulated voice, hair or other striking physical features.

As you study the change curve diagram below, you may remember that Lucy got stuck between feeling anger and denial. She also sometimes felt like blaming others for all her problems, but kept going round in circles between these three stages. Longer-term, fear prevented her from taking any bold steps to improve her situation, and it was only after she worked with her coach and began to understand the reasons behind it all that she could move through to understanding and acceptance.

Exercise: Change

- Think of a time that you went through a significant transition – do you recognise elements from the change curve diagram? Ask yourself what you are feeling now. Do any of the particular elements match up? For example, really thinking you were going to get that part then being shocked and dismayed to be turned down, followed by feeling angry with the casting director and looking for someone to blame?

- In future, when you feel stuck and disempowered, ask yourself where you are on the change curve. Look back and try to work out if you have already experienced some of the stages, such as having been in denial that your career is not really progressing, but now feeling really fearful that it's never going to work out?

- Show this diagram to a few friends that you trust. Ask them to challenge you as to where you are on the curve the next time you are struggling to come to terms with a change in your life, and offer to do the same for them.

'Awareness is curative'
Know where you are on the curve

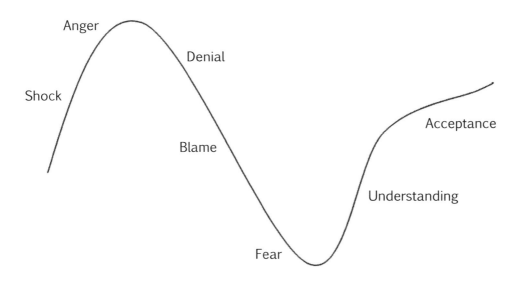

Summary

The mind–body connection is far more powerful than most people recognise. Raising awareness of your emotional and physical states and putting practices in place to help you regulate these will improve your well-being and resilience.

1 Brown, Swart & Meyler, *Emotional Intelligence* (in the *Neuroleadership Journal*, 2009)

2 W. Timothy Gallwey, *The Inner Game of Tennis* (Pan Books, 1986)

Personality Perspectives

8

Who am I today?

There are some situations in which we all perform well, and some situations in which we struggle. Some people struggle with tasks which demand a meticulous attention to detail, and prefer to do something more creative or imaginative. For others, the opposite is true. It is important to play to your strengths, while at the same time building on your weaknesses. Knowing how you perform in different contexts can be a key to success. This knowledge can make you feel bolder and more confident when you are operating within secure boundaries, and it can also help you to adapt when you are outside your comfort zone. This self-awareness and self-regulation are the cornerstones of emotional intelligence. The guidance in this chapter will help you to improve on your self-awareness and emotional intelligence, and therefore improve on the way you behave and perform in a variety of contexts.

You may know some people who always seem to say the right thing, and appear comfortable in any situation. They seem to behave with grace and integrity at all times. You may wish to emulate this type of behaviour, and it is advisable to work on elements of your behaviour from within in order to appear more 'together', calm or 'in control'. Starting with yourself is the best strategy, and so we will look at a way of breaking down complex patterns of behaviour into something simpler. This will help your

Your vision will become clear only when you can look into your own heart.

Who looks outside, dreams; who looks inside, awakes.

C. G. Jung

feelings and emotions to become more manageable, so that you feel like you can actually begin to deal with these patterns and either relish them or initiate some change. By doing the exercises in this chapter, you are going to:

o Reflect on your personality as a working actor, and how you present yourself.

o Become aware of the preferences in the way your brain naturally works.

o Acquire a better understanding of what is going on in your mind, and how you can use this information to appear to become the most effective, creative, well-rounded and successful person that you can be.

'Personality' is a tricky thing to define. It often seems changeable and fluid. The individual parts that comprise personality can be difficult to pin down. The exercises in this chapter will certainly require some reflection, but this effort will then make more practical matters seem easier to deal with.

The concept behind this first exercise is based on the premise that our personalities are made up of about six different sub-types.[1] Personality is probably a mixture of genes and the life experiences during our formative years which shape us as adults. It is the characteristic patterns of thoughts, feelings and behaviours that make us unique. If we can distinguish the sub-types of our personality and name them as if they were distinct personae or characters, it will help us to get to know the patterns of how we tend to react in certain situations. This awareness will improve our emotional intelligence, and our behaviour in different contexts will become easier to understand.

With improved self-awareness, time and practice, we can take charge of who we are and choose the response that will be most beneficial. This is not an exercise in impersonation. It is a way of viewing the variety of different ways that you reveal yourself to the world. These different aspects to your personality are all authentic elements of who you are. Authenticity is a highly attractive quality, and revealing your authentic self is often a key to success.

Let us explore the notion of sub-personalities before we look at the exercise in more detail. We all have a dominant personality style. This is not about roles you play in life: mother, father, brother, sister, husband, wife, actor or teacher, but about the way that you are as a person. Looking at Lucy's sub-personalities will help to explore this.

Lucy's dominant personality trait is *The Chameleon* – she is good at morphing and behaving how she thinks the people around want her to be. She does this quite naturally; she is well-liked and fits easily into most social situations. She even dresses quite differently according to the setting she is anticipating. Sometimes this is on purpose, and sometimes she seems to do it intuitively without consciously realising.

Her second strongest personality type is *The Show-off* – she would never like to be underdressed compared to other women in the room. This is the Lucy that believes she will make it as an actor and sees herself as attractive, talented and special. In this mode, she seeks to be the centre of attention; she is vivacious and energetic and tends to be the most proactive in terms of trying to progress her career. As this tends to be quite an extrovert character, she doesn't usually stay in this mode for long periods of time.

At times, she can be a bit of a *Princess* – she can become quite aloof and demanding; expecting good things to come to her but not really prepared to put the work in to make this happen. She is not often like this but this trait can come out when she is feeling the pressure or starting to doubt herself. Her closest friends and family have come to recognise these phases.

When really going through a bad time and feeling helpless, Lucy turns on *The Damsel in Distress*. Although she can be quite resourceful at these times in finding the right people to help her with whatever her current crisis is, she tends to expect others to sort her problems out rather than believing she can do much herself. She uses her feminine wiles to achieve the right solutions for herself. Once things improve, she tends to snap out of this way of being, quite quickly. Increasingly she is learning from it and becoming more independent and capable over time. With the ups and downs of her fledgling career, she does find it quite hard at times not to get into this slightly victim-like state of being.

Another major character for Lucy is *The Dreamer* – in this mode, Lucy can spend a lot of time thinking about what could be or what might have been, and wondering why some actors achieve success when she has not yet. She might compare herself favourably to a famous actor and think that she could have played the part better, but not actually think about the reasons that the situation is as it is. She dwells on what events and attributes have led others to success, but in this dream-like state, she doesn't consider that her own actions might also affect the outcome. *The Dreamer* is a very inert state of being and Lucy rarely acts on these thoughts to do anything productive about achieving her dream.

These are Lucy's five main modes of operating, and she can identify the situations in which they come to the fore. However, there are two more which appear less frequently.

One extreme of her personality, which sometimes manifests itself, is *The Vamp*. This is a darker side to Lucy's character in which she is prepared to trade on her sexual and emotional energy to get what she wants. This can range from simple flirting to more destructive behaviour. It may be a maladaptive way of boosting low self-esteem after either a personal or professional disappointment. Clearly, behaving in this way has been reinforced by it being successful at times. Lucy is aware that she needs to tone this down – it can lead to the wrong impression and she would aim to behave in a more professional way.

Finally, Lucy can become *The Carer*. In this mode she can almost lose herself in someone else's problems and issues. On the one hand, this makes Lucy a terrific support to people, but on the other hand, she can sometimes become so involved in others' lives that she does not concentrate on her own agenda for days at a time.

Margaret also spent some time exploring her sub-personalities. On reflection, she discovered: *The Earth Mother*, *The Lush Bohemian*, *The Dinner-party Hostess*, *The Rageful Rumpelstiltskin* and *The Matron*.

These aspects of their psyches coexist in Lucy and Margaret at all times, but come to the fore more or less at different times, depending on a variety of internal and external factors. Do you recognise any of these traits in yourself? Having read about Lucy and Margaret, are you starting to identify the ways that you can behave?

The following exercise will help you to formulate your own sub-personalities.

Exercise: Sub-personalities

Get a pen and paper and sit by yourself or with a friend and ask yourself the following questions:

● What is my dominant personality trait? Most people hesitate at this point but it is the most important part: just plunge in and write something down – like most tasks, it gets easier once you have started (if you need help, refer to the examples of Lucy and Margaret).

● Give it a name as if it were a character, and record a basic description of that character to make it more recognisable to your conscious mind (e.g. *The Chameleon* or *The Dreamer*).

● Go through, repeating this exercise until you (and your friend) think you have addressed each aspect of your personality (as mentioned, this is usually six).

● If you are struggling at any point, remember that sub-personalities often have an opposite pairing – for example, *The Show-off* and *The Damsel in Distress* – so it might be helpful to work out what these pairs might be.

● Do not be afraid to address dark parts of yourself that you are not necessarily proud of. This exercise can often release some of the negativity held around these feelings.

This exercise does not have to be completed at once. It can remain as a work in progress while you continue to read this book. It is important that you understand which situations automatically trigger which of your sub-personalities. How do you reveal yourself according to different situations, people or events? For example, who are you when you:

● Go to a party?

- Work in an office?
- Interact with your parents?
- Go to an audition?

Once you have established your basic sub-personalities, you may want to look again at and revise this list every six months or every year. It can be amazing how a sub-personality might decline as it becomes less needed, and another might be formed and appear for certain situations. Reflecting often will help you to understand how and why you are behaving in certain ways, and over time the basic constants will become clear.

Once you have a notion of who you become in different situations, you can begin to understand each sub-personality and their dynamics better. You can start to utilise each personality perspective to its full potential and use the information you now have to manage any downsides. If necessary, you can even learn new ways of 'being' that are not your natural inclination, but may serve you better in your purpose of becoming a jobbing actor. Lucy calls this her 'professional hat', and although this may sound superficial, she has been working hard to create new habits that become part of her repertoire, effectively adding to and subtracting from alternative personality types to enhance her natural strengths. She sees this as playing around with her options rather than dwelling on it too seriously or over-analysing herself. Lucy worked out that *The Show-off* actually serves her best when going to auditions, and that depending on whom she might be seeing (her agent, a director, other actors), she benefits from the expertise of *The Chameleon*. She has recently also been trying to move away from being *The Damsel in Distress* as she recognises this is not helpful for her, and introduce a new character aspect called *The Tomboy*. This new sub-personality helps her to engage with friends and other actors of both genders in a new and positive way, and balances out her *Princess* side. *The Vamp* is a part of her that she does not experience any benefit from and she is working to turn it into *The Steady Young Woman*. She also realises that no one is perfect and that the journey of self-discovery is important in itself so she has stopped rebuking herself if she lapses into *The Vamp* from time to time and just starts afresh the next day. So *The Tomboy* and *The Steady Young Woman* will hopefully be integrated into her true personality over time. This may be harder to do without the help of a coach, mentor or psychologist.

You may want to reflect on when your sub-personalities tend to surface and how you can ensure that they present themselves only at the most helpful times. The following exercise will add depth to the findings from the sub-personalities exercise.

Exercise: Professional persona

Go back to the list of sub-personalities you identified. Do this exercise when you know you will have a decent amount of uninterrupted time to yourself. Ask yourself the following questions about each character. Self-knowledge and reflection are the important factors here – this is not about becoming something you are not.

1   When does this character appear? In which situations? Around whom? In which of your moods?

2   How does this character appear? Raise your awareness of how this feeling starts physically in your body then manifests itself in how you think, and how you feel. How do these work together to affect how you behave? You may want a creative way of representing this: digitally alter or draw onto pictures of yourself to represent how you change for each character.

---

3   How does this character hinder you? Think particularly about meetings here, as these are high-pressure situations where you will tend to default to automatic behaviours and attitudes.

4   How does this character help you? Note down times that you have been proud of the way you have handled a situation, and felt resilient due to the traits of this character.

5   Which combinations or proportions of characters do you think would be effective in meetings?

6   Which sub-personalities would you suppress during a meeting if you could?

7   Where does there seem to be a gap in helpful personality aspects that you could incorporate into your professional persona? Are there any other characters that you could usefully develop?

Exercise: Who do you defer to?

There is a very powerful question which is linked to sub-personalities. This will help you decide how you might most effectively strengthen your persona. Ask yourself whose opinions you usually submit to or to whose authority you make yourself subservient. Whom are you reluctant to challenge, provoke or disagree with?

Lucy worked out that she tends to defer to older, male, more experienced actors and directors. This formerly unconscious psychological process was leading to her bringing out *The Princess* or *The Damsel in Distress* or even *The Vamp* when in the presence of such people and this was not doing her any favours. At times of feeling disadvantaged in some way, she needed to call on *The Show-off* and *The Tomboy* more than ever, rather than default to her usual response.

Continue with the exercise to reflect and build even further on knowing yourself through your sub-personalities. As mentioned previously, this reflection is to be thought of as a work in progress because more and more answers to these questions will occur to you over time.

When you are aware to whom you defer, ask yourself the following questions:

- What is it about these people that make you feel this way (this may relate to childhood experiences or social expectation)?

- Which personalities emerge in the presence of these types of people?

- Is behaving in this way serving you in the short-term? Is it useful in the long-term?

- What reaction might the way you are behaving provoke in the other person – is this a good thing or unhelpful?

- What shifts could you make and how would this help?

Beginning to understand how and why you behave in different ways to different people in various contexts will lead to a more professional way of behaving, a more controlled presentation, and will help to lead you to becoming the responsible person that you want to be.

NeuroSynthesis

Now, let us move from the psychological to the neuroscientific. The diagram below is the NeuroSynthesis model (adapted by Tara Swart from Roberto Assagioli). It divides up the *modus operandi* of the professional actor into six branches in order to maximise productivity. It assigns certain parts of the brain (in bold) to each of these ways of operating (above them). An important foundation to understanding your mind is through understanding the mechanics of how your brain works in your professional practice.

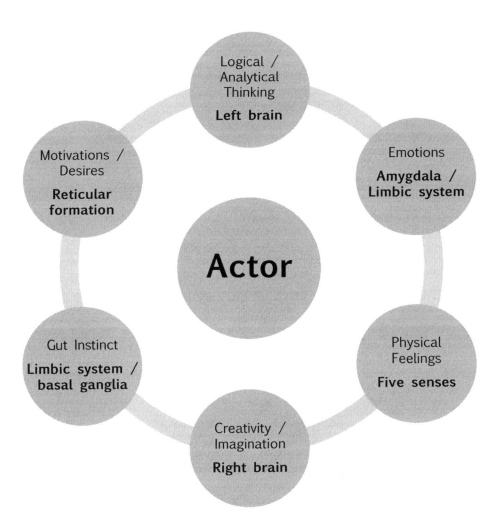

If you can bring together the several aspects in the diagram to optimal effect, you will be operating at your most effective. So, for example, if you naturally tend to be creative and intuitive, how might you improve your performance by tapping into feedback from your physical feelings or logic?

The way our brains work when we are doing our job is through a combination of the processes indicated in the six boxes in the diagram which feed into the centre:

o   Thinking (logical/analytical) which is commonly regarded as occurring mostly in the left side of the brain (in right-handed people).

o   Emotional feelings which are mediated in a part of the brain called the amygdala or limbic system.

o   Physical feelings, by which we mean feedback from the body though the senses.

o   Creativity or imagination which is commonly thought to be found in the right side of the brain (in right-handed people) – this can be about using metaphor and analogy or visual concepts to look at things differently.

o   Intuition or our 'sixth sense', which may be felt by some people as their gut instinct. Gut instinct alone may not lead to better decisions, but in combination with what we know, it can be a very powerful tool to bring the unknown into the known.

o   Awareness of our motivation or our drives and desires for a certain outcome also affect how we operate, and this is believed to be mediated by the Reticular Activating System deep in the brain, which is also responsible for sleep-wake cycles and drives for hunger, thirst, libido.

> **Exercise: NeuroSynthesis**
>
> Have a good look at the diagram on page 111, and the list of brain functions. Imagine yourself at the centre of it. Think about your attitude to work and how you handle your career and:
>
> - Score yourself from zero to ten for each of the brain functions in terms of how effective you consider yourself to be (0 is the least effective, 10 is the most effective).
>
> - Examine the patterns – are you fairly consistent across the functions or are there significant gaps?
>
> - Commit to one thing you can do each week for the next few weeks to try to build on your strengths, as well as your development areas (the lower-scoring brain functions).

Here are Lucy's scores according to how effective she is at various ways of working. The scores are out of 10:

→ Thinking (logical/analytical)   5

→ Emotional feelings   8

→ Physical feelings   4

→ Creativity or imagination   9

→ Intuition or 'sixth sense'   9

→ Awareness of motivation or drives   4

As we can see, Lucy considers herself to be weaker at working with physical feelings, and awareness of motivation. She sees herself as average in the area of thinking and analysing, and good with her emotional feelings, her creativity and her intuition. With this information, Lucy is now in a position to reflect on her strengths and weaknesses, and concentrate on those areas which might lead to working in a more effective and balanced way.

For example, in order to increase her score for 'Thinking (logical/analytical)', Lucy started to read some books about acting. She also kept a daily record of her thoughts as she reflected on professional events and occurrences. In order to improve her physical awareness, she took up a yoga class. Finally, in order to improve her awareness of her motivation, Lucy ensured that she was eating and sleeping regularly, and she became mindful of the impulses behind her actions, especially when she was seeking deliberate distractions such as gossiping with a friend or idly looking at videos on YouTube.

Here are some other ways of improving your brain-function scores:

Thinking (logical/analytical)

o   Read books relevant to your craft, or study an approach to acting which is new to you: Uta Hagen or Sanford Meisner, for example.

o   Read a biography of an actor or artist you admire and reflect on similarities to or differences from your own life and attitudes.

o   When asked to make an important decision, see if you can distinguish between what your head is thinking and what your intuition is urging. Try to imagine the outcome if you were to follow your head rather than your heart. Would you surprise yourself or others if you acted in this way?

Emotional feeling

o   Redo the self-awareness exercise in Chapter 7, page 94 (Raising awareness of how you are feeling emotionally, mentally and physically).

o   Sit and write a reflection about what you are feeling. Only write about your feelings, rather than events or people. Do this for fifteen minutes a day for a few days, and reflect on whether it changes your awareness of yourself in everyday situations.

Physical feeling

o   Redo the self-care/unblocking creativity exercise in Chapter 7, page 98.

o   Whenever you blush, laugh nervously or feel goose bumps, ask yourself what this might mean and use this information to guide you.

o   Spend some time focusing on the physical sensations you may be experiencing: warmth, cold, tastes, smells, ease of sitting or standing, discomfort, hunger, physical well-being.

Imagination

o   Explore a creative medium that is not usually yours: perhaps writing or sculpting or singing.

o   Write a hypothetical magazine article charting your successful career.

o   Create a clay model of yourself as a successful actor; or make a collage of your life from photos or drawings.

o   Choose a character from a play and write a first-person monologue from this character's perspective. Set the monologue a year before the play begins, or a year after the play ends.

Intuition

o   Tap into your feelings, look for 'signs' in your life that might give you guidance.

o   Follow your heart instead of your head sometimes and see what kind of results you get. If this is outside your comfort zone, only try it on low-impact decisions at first. Why not allow the more intuitive version of yourself to reign free at a networking event? How do other people's reactions compare to how you would normally be received?

Awareness of motivation

o   Ask yourself what the real agenda behind what you are doing or trying to do is. What is it that motivates or demotivates you? What are your hopes and fears? Make a note of these and revisit and update them.

o   Examine your interactions with different types of people more closely – who motivates you positively and who does not? Who puts your art at the forefront of your mind and who puts competition to the fore?

o   What are some of your peers' motivations for doing what they do?

o   Make weekly lists of action points and set goals every three months.

Summary

With these exercises, you may have had some pleasant surprises, and you might have seen some things you did not like the look of. By the end of this book you will have an opportunity to reconstruct your thought processes and challenge your tacit decision-making. Start building this capability into your toolkit by breaking down all the practical matters you come across that seem a little too difficult or overwhelming, and handle them by looking at them in bite-sized pieces. By thinking more creatively, by multitasking in a new way, or bringing extra resources into your life, you will be able to develop new behaviour patterns and bring the best of those into building up an effective professional persona.

1 Piero Ferrucci, *What We May Be: Techniques for Psychological and Spiritual Growth* (Jeremy P. Tarcher, 2000)

Keeping Connected 9

Creative communities and tribes

> *Tribe: a social group bound by common ancestry and ties of consanguinity and affinity; a common language and territory; and characterised by a political and economic organisation.*
>
> *Ken Robinson*, The Element[1]

Call it a clan, call it a network, call it a tribe, call it a family. Whatever you call it, whoever you are, you need one.

Jane Howard

For most people, a primary component of being in their element is connecting with other people who share their passion and a desire to make the most of themselves through it.

Although a sense of community can be a large part of the reason that people turn to theatre, television and film for their careers, the reality can be surprisingly lonely, particularly between jobs or at different stages in your career. In any disconcerting or unknown situation, the restorative nature of 'support groups' is highly commended by people from all walks of life: everything from Alcoholics Anonymous to bereavement support groups or antenatal classes. So, why not a tribe for actors?

Today we are not bound by ancient rules of clans and kinship, but are more free to choose our friends, partners and colleagues. There are pros and cons to modern social structure, and although downsides may be the loss of community, social bonding and nurture, a concomitant bonus is freedom of choice. These choices include the chance to build our own tribes and communities that are not based on blood relationships but on common passions and values. Within this, there is an understanding that we will support each other through failures and celebrate each other's successes. For the purposes of this chapter, we are not going to discuss social groups or friendships but tribes of professional, like-minded people with a common purpose or talent: actors, directors, writers, producers, designers – creative people generally.

Ken Robinson goes on to say:

> *Connecting with people who share the same passions affirms that you're not alone; that there are others like you and that, while many might not understand your passion, some do... What matters first is having validation for the passion you have in common.*

Finding a group of like-minded people with empathy and perspective for your situation brings all sorts of opportunities for sharing ideas, getting other people's perspective on things, helping each other out, and knowing you have people to turn to in good times and bad. It can be very inspiring to hear from people who have been through the same things that you might be experiencing now. Indeed, you might be able to offer the benefits of your experience to others – not only can this be rewarding, but you should listen to the advice you give to others and challenge yourself as to whether you are taking it yourself.

Tara: My tribe has been going for eighteen months now. The idea came from a friend and associate, Rachel, another coach who works exclusively in the creative industries. She told me about the book, The Element, and the accompanying TED talk: http://tinyurl.com/24qxfl4

It stated that:

> *Finding your tribe can have transformative effects on your sense of identity and purpose. This is because of three powerful tribal dynamics: validation, inspiration, and what he calls the alchemy of synergy.*

As executive coaches, these ideas were appealing to us, so we decided to invite a couple of people each and see how it could grow. We toyed with the idea of inviting only other coaches at first, but in the end decided the most benefit would come from widening it to being a creative community for freelance women. Between us, we initially included a couple of other coaches, a sculptor and a graphic designer. We asked each interested party to invite someone they thought would be a great addition to our tribe. Our tribe then also included an interior designer, an art curator and an acupuncturist. This tribe is a group of women of various ages that I am proud to be associated with, and we have continued to meet once a month at various locations, with one of us taking responsibility for making it happen each time. Our agreement is that at least five members need to be able to attend each meeting to make it worthwhile. We do a general update on our progress since the last meeting, for about five minutes each, and then whoever has a pressing issue that they need input on gets to be the focus of an 'action learning set' (see below).

We made the decision to stick to one gender, but this was a purely personal choice at the time and there is flexibility to create the type of tribe that suits you. The general concept is helpful for anyone who is open to receiving objective feedback from a panel of people they trust and respect, and who can be part of or outside of their normal social or professional circle, i.e. actors you did not know previously as well as your own friends, etc. Some of our tribe members are friends or colleagues independently, but most were taken on trust as they had been recommended or invited by someone else in the group.

Exercise: Action learning set

This exercise is best done with a group of at least four – one person to be the subject and three or more people to act as the panel.

- The subject describes their issue or dilemma for 5–10 minutes without interruption. This may be around work/life balance, PR, financial issues, dealing with stress, etc.

- They are then open to questions from the group for about 10 minutes – each person should be able to ask at least one question.

- For the following 15–20 minutes, the subject gets the opportunity to sit back, listen and take notes, while the group discusses possible solutions and explores options that may not have been thought of previously. This can be done from a point of view of 'This is what I would do if I were X' or 'Have they thought of…?'

- At the end of that time, the particular tribe member looks at their notes from the suggestions, and makes a commitment to certain action points over the next month, which are to be reported back to the group by email within a specified time (usually 1–2 weeks if the meetings are monthly).

- The process is completed by each member of the group thanking each other – this is a very important part of the process.

A tribe would have been beneficial to Margaret, who was introduced in Chapter 1. Younger artists and creatives would have benefited from her experience and perspective, and she would have found the younger members' energy and creativity refreshing and inspiring. There would have been a place where Margaret could have regularly gone to find nurture, support and reassurance.

Your tribe may even help to protect your psychological well-being, especially if you are experiencing periods of unemployment. In 1958, Marie Jahoda developed the theory of Ideal Mental Health. She identified five categories which she said were vital to feelings of well-being (these became seen as important again in 1982 and 1987 when unemployment in the UK peaked). These were:

o   Time structure – having some sort of routine or at least a reason to get out of bed in the morning.

o   Social contact – having a decent amount of interaction with other adults at regular intervals.

o   Collective effort or purpose – being part of something meaningful.

o   Social identity or status – recognition for something beneficial you have to offer.

o   Regular activity – mental, physical and social things to do.

She maintained that people who were unemployed were deprived of these and that this accounted for much of the reported mental ill-health among the unemployed. But these same factors are equally valid for people who work freelance or independently as they are for the unemployed, especially in a profession such as acting where work and money can be irregular and infrequent. You can build your tribe to provide all or many of these structures and activities for you, which could be especially important in the time between jobs for actors.

Take some time to think about the five categories above. How are these categories represented in your life, or if they are not, what is the effect on you of their being neglected? What measures could you put into place to ensure each category becomes a part of your core stability, that is, the resources deep within you that keep you strong?

There are other ways of benefiting from the security of a tribe or a community, and experiencing this support and nurturing. Other ideas suitable for creative communities include:

o   Online forums such as groups on social networking sites – there are already many groups for actors to join on Facebook and LinkedIn, but you can set up your own group on Google or Yahoo for posting queries, advice and events.

o   In addition to meeting your tribe face to face, using virtual media such as the artsjobs and artsnews websites, and also the various subscription-based online web services for casting can be useful.

o   Dining club – a group who meet regularly for dinner – costs can be kept down by cooking and hosting at each other's homes. This is similar in structure to a tribe but involves food, and is perhaps less prescriptive in its format. Usually these are purely social in nature, but can be made professionally relevant by inviting guest speakers or having some form of presentation. (See the anecdote from Tara below.)

o   Book club – meetings centred around reading and/or reviewing plays, or books for actors.

o   Networking events (these could be held annually by your tribe to expand your network). This is where people invite others that are not known to the group as their guest – all the better if this someone is a producer, director or writer. Many of you might know someone with a particular area of expertise who would be happy to address your group at no cost.

o   An organised group of people who regularly attend events together. Going to the theatre or cinema could seem a less effective event for actors as it might feel a bit like a busman's holiday. However, going to a public lecture or art exhibition can often help you to feel refreshed and stimulated. Many theatres and galleries arrange wide-ranging platform events and talks to complement their productions or exhibitions. You will also meet like-minded people who are open to chat after these events, so you may also expand your network or community.

Tara: I was invited to join a dining club that had the following format: people were invited to meet four times a year at a fixed location that could provide food. This one was at a private members' club but private rooms at gastro-pubs are often hired out at no charge. Equal numbers of men and women were invited to become members, and if you could not attend one of the meetings, you had to send an alter ego of the same gender in your place. Each time, one of the members was responsible for inviting a guest speaker relevant to the profession. As it happens, I did not join it for several reasons: the cost was high; I could already see that I would not be able to make two of the dates; most of the other people that were to be members were people that I saw regularly anyway so I did not feel that the investment would expand my network sufficiently; I already have my tribe and regularly attend a variety of networking events. However, I thought it was a great idea, and as they ended up attracting members that were not usually a part of their social or professional circle, it has turned out to be a great success.

There is a danger for actors in creating these networks. There is little point in involving yourself with actors who are at a similar stage as you are in your career, or even feeling similarly frustrated. It is important that you diversify, and invite a broad range of people who work in the creative industries, and a wide range of ages is also recommended. It is important that a diverse range of experience is available to the group.

Andrew: I have a friend who came to London from Australia, and he felt that he needed to create a network around him. He initiated a monthly networking event for people who worked in the television industry. He would organise the venue, and ensure that there was a bar and food available. The only condition was that each person who came brought someone who had never been to these events before. After a year or so, he decided to stop organising these events: they had become too popular and time-consuming. He also felt that he had now met enough people!

In his excellent book, *Never Eat Alone*, Keith Ferrazzi explains the importance of sharing your contacts and allowing your networks to expand.[2] This typically positive North American approach can teach reserved Brits and Europeans something significant. When a network is shared, its impact and efficacy is doubled. When we are in a positive and healthy state of mind, we all enjoy introducing people to each other; it makes us feel useful, connected, and part of a larger community. People enjoy sharing their friends and contacts, though some assume wrongly that creating a new connection between two people will leave them disempowered and left out. As counterintuitive as this may seem, the opposite is true: gratitude and celebration of a new relationship will mean that you are always connected to these people.

When you think about people you know who are successful, it is likely that you will also discover that these are the people who are generous with their networks and contacts. They fearlessly make introductions and selflessly help out in the knowledge that a network shared is a network extended.

Incidentally, Keith Ferrazzi rarely uses the terms 'network' or 'networking' in his book. He talks of 'communities' and 'community-building'. These are useful terms as they remind us of the generosity of a community of people helping each other, rather than any selfish and expedient implications of the word 'networking'.

If you have read Malcolm Gladwell's *The Tipping Point*,[3] you will know that people who seem to instinctively build communities – or 'connectors' as he calls them – are instrumental in making epidemics happen: the popularity of iPhones; the campaign to make Rage Against the Machine the Christmas Number One; the queues to get tickets for Jez Butterworth's play *Jerusalem* at four in the morning. These are all events that have depended on the efficacy of connectors. This can also be applied to an actor's career. If an actor is present in enough networks and an active member in a big-enough community, then he or she will always spring to mind when there is a job on offer – especially when that job is being cast in a hurry, perhaps because someone has dropped out – and as we know, this is often the reason for someone getting work.

Exercise: Your tribe

- Think of two or three people that you could usefully form a tribe with. Consider demographics such as age, gender, profession, stage of progress within that profession, family status, a theme such as 'creatives' or 'freelancers'.

- Approach these people with your idea and ask them if they find it interesting, and if so, whether they can think of further people to invite.

- Get a reasonable number of people together and arrange to meet up and explore how you might take things forward.

- Try out an 'action learning set' or come up with some ideas for interesting guests you might invite.

Summary

Neither the negative impact of isolation nor the benefits of a community can be underestimated. Loneliness, inertia and despondency can all be relieved by simply having the support of a group who understand. While sympathetic friends are always a help, a structured and regular facility for support is essential. Tribe meetings, networking events and public lectures are all valuable and effective methods of keeping yourself connected and feeling vibrant.

1 Ken Robinson, with Lou Aronica, *The Element: How Finding Your Passion Changes Everything* (Allen Lane, 2009)

2 Keith Ferrazzi, *Never Eat Alone* (Doubleday Business, 2005)

3 Malcolm Gladwell, *The Tipping Point* (Abacus, 2001)

Planning for Success **10**

What does success mean to you? What will it look like, feel like and sound like? Having a well-thought-out vision of success is much more likely to lead you to it than if you are wandering relatively aimlessly along the path of being an aspiring actor. Success means something different for different people, and it is important that you define what you mean by success in order to visualise it fully. For some actors, success is one paid theatre job a year; for others it might be three film roles. Some actors view artistic satisfaction as their reward; for others it is fame and fortune. Whether your motivation is artistic reward, material success or a need to be recognised, it is important that you are clear and honest with yourself. This is not a matter for being judgemental.

Tara: After seven years as a doctor, I decided to change career, and worked for a boutique management-consulting firm whilst doing my executive-coach training. At the end of six months I was faced with a decision as to whether to try and stay in the consulting job or start my own coaching business. As I tried to visualise a career in consulting, I was repeatedly met with the image of the steepest, darkest hill I had ever seen. When I imagined myself as a successful coach in three years' time, I saw an image of my life with balance and variety – the flexibility to work alone and in association with others; from home and in large offices; the opportunity to write some articles (or even a book) and keep up with the literature regarding trends in the coaching industry, so that I could continue to offer my clients innovative ideas. I saw myself spending most of my time coaching

Always bear in mind that your own resolution to succeed is more important than any one thing.

Abraham Lincoln

clients and enjoying it immensely, but also networking a lot and being a success at running the business side of things. I saw myself earning more money than I ever did as a doctor. I felt relaxed and content.

Taking your vision and structuring plans with milestones to ensure that you achieve it, is likely to improve your chances yet further. We believe that it is important to define what it is that you want, both in a practical way and in terms of feelings, so define your success in terms of how it will be for you, and in terms of what you want to have achieved within a certain time scale. You can have your heart set on something but fail to achieve it if your mind is not focused. Equally, if you have an external idea of what success is, but it does not appeal authentically to you, it will make it more difficult to achieve, and ultimately may not be fulfilling for you as a person or as an actor.

Exercise: Brand values

One way of looking at this is by considering your 'brand values' – you need to decide what your values are as an artist, as this can often help in making decisions about the direction to go in when logic alone does not give a complete answer. We have come up with the following suggestions, but many other values exist. It is important that you come up with a list that is meaningful to you. Don't move on until you have done this. Actually write the list down, don't just do it in your head.

- Integrity – this is your moral code. Have you defined where your own moral boundaries lie? Are you trustworthy, discerning and careful? What does integrity mean to you?

- Professionalism – here we include the discipline and focus to succeed in your chosen career. Are you someone whose professional conduct makes them sought after?

- Authenticity – being true to yourself.

- Sustainability – this lends itself to a career with longevity.

- Determination – are dedication and focus qualities that you value? Or is 'determination' a dirty word for you? Quiet assurance and determination, rather than persistence, can actually be attractive qualities.

Generally I have the career I have chosen myself.

Damian Lewis

Exercise: Vision board

Take five minutes in a quiet space to visualise what success beyond your wildest dreams would be for you. Imagine yourself at a certain age, in a certain number of years, having achieved your goals. Where will you be living and who will you be surrounded by? What factors will make it apparent to you that you have achieved success? Once you have savoured this image in your mind and body, let the feeling sink in. Peruse images in magazines or on the internet that strike a chord with what you have envisaged.

- Have a pin board or a large piece of thick card you can stick some images onto. Have scissors and glue at the ready.

- Select and cut out the images or phrases that appeal to you.

- Lay them out on the card. Some images will immediately feel out of place and these can be discarded. Keep going until you have filled the space with images that fit your picture of success, then glue them into position.

- Place this board in a prominent place that you can see every day (if you don't want everyone else to see it then you can put it inside your wardrobe or as a screensaver on your computer

> or smartphone, but there shouldn't be anything on it that you will not be proud to achieve and having people know what your goals are can help you achieve them too). Reflect on what the overall picture projects: critical acclaim, happiness, satisfaction, selfishness, balance?
>
> - Redo this exercise after six months to monitor your progress and check that these are all still the things that you want.

As well as representing your vision pictorially, it is wise to record it in a document such as a business plan. If you keep this in digital format on your computer or phone, it can easily be altered over time, and successive versions can be saved so that you can also look back and chart your progress. Many creative people baulk at the idea of writing a business plan, but we have reiterated in this book that as an actor, *you* are your business, and success is connected to treating yourself as such. You can think of it as a personal-development plan or career-path plan, and make your document suit you – it could be a list or an essay.

Exercise: Business plan

Construct your personal career-path plan by following these headings:

- *Vision* – one or two sentences to capture where you see yourself in five years' time. For example, 'I have a reputation as an actor working in television and theatre, who is reliable, creative and exciting. When the part of a mid-thirties regular and likeable guy is being cast, I am the first actor to come to mind.'

- *Mission* – three or four bullet points about what you specifically wish to achieve. This could include the kind of work you are doing, level of public acclaim or how much money you earn. For example, 'I have several good pieces of work behind me each year that lead to regular meetings; I earn enough money from theatre, television and voice-over work that I do not need to take on other employment; I am occasionally interviewed.'

- *Strategy* – how you achieve the above: 'I get a good agent that represents me well in the areas in which I wish to focus; I contact and meet at least one key influential person every month; I keep up with the latest news on what is being cast.'

- *Tactics* – the things you do to maintain your strategy: 'I keep in touch regularly with people that influence my career options; I stay fit, healthy and well-rested so that I turn up reliably to auditions, and people like working with me.'

- *Targets* – for example, 'Three pieces of paid work per year (specify whether television, theatre, film, adverts); twenty auditions a year; two pieces of unpaid work I really enjoy/learn from/meet new people at.'

- *Stretch targets* – these are targets that it would be great to achieve over and above the targets that you realistically need to maintain your career as an actor. For example, 'All of the above plus another two pieces of paid work per year (a total of five).'

- *Project management* – this is about organising and managing your time in the search for work. This includes keeping up with your business plan; doing the exercises in this book regularly; reading generally (specify how many books per year); networking or 'community-building' (how many events will you attend? How many key people will you arrange to meet?); and may include specifics around physical exercise, getting good headshots and refining your brand.

- *Personal development* – this includes things like reading this book or going on a course to improve your technical skills or attitude. Andrew and Tara run courses several times a year, also called *An Attitude for Acting*, which many actors have benefited from already. (See their website www.attitude4acting.co.uk)

- *Finances* – work out how much you need to earn to cover your expenses. Look at how much you are earning from any part-time work, indirectly or not linked to your craft, and how much you are earning from acting. How much would you need to earn from acting in order not to have to do other work? Where can you cut costs and where can you generate earnings? How much would you have to earn to be debt-free? How much to be comfortable? How much to be well-off? How much would you like to be earning in five years' time? Break down an annual salary into how much you need to be bringing in each month. Stick this number to your vision board.

- *Marketing* – gather information from the internet and subscription services, your agent, other actors, books and magazines about what is out there. Keep your network up-to-date with what you are aiming for.

- *Selling* – you cannot sell yourself as an actor if you do not know what you are selling. Practise your 'sales pitch' at every opportunity – informally with friends and family as well as chasing up potential meetings and key people with phone calls. Refine the art of appearing confident but not arrogant. Although not aimed at the creative sector, Richard Denny's excellent book, *Selling to Win*, includes techniques for maintaining your confidence in the face of negativity where the temptation may be to slip into inertia.[1]

Tara: I revise my business plan every three months. I make a plan for the year in January, then look at it and adjust it in April, July and October. I ask myself if the plan still reflects the direction in which I want my business to go. Have I reached my targets for the previous three months? If not, why not, and if so, what made this happen and how can this continue to be cultivated? Has anything unexpected happened that might warrant a shift in the emphasis of where I might best be employing my energy and focus? Is this still the right thing for me to be doing?

Some people would argue that giving up is the only form of failure, and that if you are prepared to persist as an actor, you will make a career of it. Many people will give up for various reasons: financial, the need to concentrate on raising a family, or having decided to do something else. Others will reason that they have to draw the line somewhere and that if they are not getting a certain amount of work or earning a certain amount of money through acting within a specified time frame, then there are other things that they can do and enjoy, whilst maintaining their desired lifestyle. These choices are highly personal and there is no right or wrong. It is important, however, to assess the situation critically before making any big decision.

Exercise: Adjusting your percentages

Visualise yourself as currently being at the beginning of a fruitful career. Where do you see yourself now as an actor? Draw this onto a large piece of paper, like flipchart paper, with coloured felt-tips or crayons. Keep the instructions for the 'Barriers to success' exercise in Chapter 2 (page 23) ready. For the first part of this exercise there are a few rules:

- At least four different colours must be used.

- No words may be used, but numbers are allowed.

- Try to avoid drawing 'stick men', but if you wish, you may draw people as a conceptual or metaphorical representation.

Once you have done this, do the 'Barriers to success' exercise from Chapter 2 for whatever you think is blocking you from achieving the success that you desire.

- Now adjust your drawing to represent yourself as a one hundred per cent successful actor.

- Finally, for a further five minutes, revisit the feeling of success you conjured up for your vision board in the first exercise of this chapter.

- Readjust your drawing for the final time to reflect your career as more successful than you imagined possible.

- Examine what it is that changes from picture to picture, and how this translates into what you can practically do to boost your career.

Now you will have come away with a document that is informed not only by logic but by creativity and imagination, and which is authentic to your values, emotional requirements and psychological motivators and drivers. There may be many things that you feel you should be doing as a result of reading this book, which you know would put you in a better position to get the kind of work that you want. But starting can sometimes be the most difficult thing to do.

Tara: The best piece of advice that I got when faced with the seemingly monumental task of starting to write up three years of research from my PhD was from the Professor of Anatomy at King's College, London. He simply said 'Write something.' That was over fifteen years ago, but I thought of it again when writing this book.

And so, we encourage you to do something similar with your acting career. *Do something.* Take the one, two or three points from this book that stand out the most to you and act on them. Why not start today? There is no time like the present. Over time, you can go back and read particular chapters as you encounter relevant situations, and each time different things may stand out for you.

Summary

Visualise what success means to you. Break it down into what you need to achieve in successive time periods to ensure that you are continually moving towards your picture of success. Critically appraise yourself against your goals and milestones, and do it regularly. Push yourself to achieve that little bit more than you thought you could. Retain flexibility within your plan to allow for opportunities and changes that may occur along the way.

1   Richard Denny, *Selling to Win* (Kogan Page, 2009)

An Attitude When Acting

11

So far we have discussed getting work, being available for work, and thinking positively about work. What about the work itself? What attitudes in the rehearsal room ensure success and satisfaction?

The main goal of any rehearsal period is to do your most effective work, remain open and trusting, and fully embrace the collaborative process. With this in mind, there are some key elements that are worth remembering.

It is possible that you are extremely nervous about starting the job: perhaps there are cast members who are impressive and whose status you find intimidating; perhaps the director has a formidable reputation; perhaps the scale of the work seems too great, or the subject matter too daunting. It is worth remembering that everyone is probably feeling this way. This is a time of new beginnings, and levels of anxiety can run high. Now is the time to remember that you were chosen for this role. There was no one the director and casting director met whom they considered to be as suitable for the part or as desirable to work with. The part is now yours, and all you have to do is engage fully with the work.

The next reassurance that you need is that you are fallible. The whole point of the rehearsal is that you are there to explore. Exploration means that you will make mistakes, and it is only

A man of genius makes no mistakes; his errors are volitional and are the portals of discovery.

James Joyce

through making these mistakes that you will learn. Apologies, shame and embarrassment are all a waste of time. It is important that you are bold enough to listen to the feedback of the director or other members of the ensemble, and adapt. Do not take anything personally and treat all comments as opportunities for growth.

Feeling that you are prepared will also help with rehearsal nerves. Whatever your preparation – historical, biographical, or simply rigorous analysis of the text – it is important that you feel prepared and ready. It is also important that you stick to your preferred method of preparing the text:

o   Do you break the text down into units?

o   Do you look at intentions, wants or what the character has to have?

o   Do you write down everything that others say about your character, and everything that your character says about themselves?

o   Do you use action words, or rhythm work?

o   Do you learn your part before rehearsals start or wait until you have input from the director and your fellow actors?

The dichotomy of the rehearsal room surrounds the nature of the process. Each actor has a different process, and each director's process is different again. This means that you always have to be aware of two elements at work: how the director is working and how your own process is complementing and accommodating this process.

Exercise: Rehearsal compatibility

Take some time to think about your own work process.
The following list involves all elements of rehearsal. All are
important and contribute to the organic growth of the
rehearsal process. However, different actors have different
priorities and ways of working. Rate the following impulses
of the rehearsal process in order of importance for you.
Don't move on until you have done this. Actually write the
ratings down, don't just do it in your head.

- The visual elements of the play – blocking on
  stage, design elements, props and furniture.

- The verbal elements of the play – how the script
  sounds.

- The relationships in the play – how each
  character is connected to the others, and how
  these bonds develop.

- The imaginative world of the play – the fictional
  universe in which the play is set.

- The information contained in the play – research
  and analysis taken from the text of the play.

- Historical information – how your biographical
  and historical research informs the process.

Observe the director over the first few days of rehearsal.
Repeat the exercise from the point of view you imagine
the director to be working from. Where do the director's
priorities seem to lie on this list?

Compare your list with that of how the director seems to
be working. Look at where you seem to score similarly.
This will serve as an important guide to how your own
process can best serve that of the director. The areas that
you both grade similarly are the ones that will be taken
care of in the rehearsal room. The areas in which there
are differences will require you to put the work in yourself,

*I am an instinctive
actress. I don't have
technique because I
never learnt any. I
do the cerebral bit
before I start. Then I
just let it be. I allow
whatever rises to rise
naturally. You are
tricking your
subconscious.*

Emma Thompson

> outside the rehearsal room, as something that is clearly important to you may be less of a priority to the director.
>
> The information that you gain from this exercise will help you in an essential task in the rehearsal room: translating what the director is asking for into your own language. Once you understand what is being required of you, you can then begin the process of ownership that rehearsal is for: infusing it with your own integrity, embedding it into your performance, and fully embodying it.

The reason that compatibility is so important is not only to ensure a smooth collaboration in this rehearsal period, but also to encourage future collaborations. A collaborative process which is harmonious, inspirational and empowering is a rare thing, and directors will call upon actors with whom they have this relationship again and again. It is important to look after the possibility of future work.

Many actors complicate what the job of the actor is when they are rehearsing. The primary hindrance to an effective attitude in rehearsal is the need for approval. There is no need to seek approval – being well-liked will not produce a better performance. The need for approval is accompanied by several bad habits:

o   Policing yourself, and blocking what is instinctive.

o   Being hesitant, rather than immediate with your creativity.

o   Waiting to be directed, rather than making offers.

o   Being too severe with yourself when you make a mistake.

o   Being too judgemental of others when they make a mistake.

o   Carrying tension in your body, rather than being free, released and in a creative state.

o   Worrying about the immediate gratification of getting approval, rather than focusing on growth in your personal rehearsal period.

Even though collaboration is essential in a rehearsal period, autonomy is the key to an effective attitude. On every level, it is important that you take responsibility for yourself. The quality and intensity of your performance is entirely down to you, and no one else. Some actors are easier to work with than others; they appear to give more, or respond more, or communicate more. These actors are, of course, a delight to work with and instil a creative rapport. However, if this rapport is not apparent, there is no reason why your process or your performance should suffer. Often in a company of actors, one actor is singled out as the one who is dull to work with, or whose fault it is that there is no life in the scene. Be wary of getting involved with this; try and remain impartial. It is highly unlikely that this actor is responsible for it all going wrong. He or she is simply being used as a scapegoat for everyone else's inadequacy, and it is important to be aware that this form of mild bullying is unfortunately common.

Andrew: As a director, I occasionally encounter this problem either at drama schools or in professional companies. An actor comes up to me and complains about another actor in a scene, and how the scene would be different if only the other actor in the scene were more responsive. I am never sympathetic. It is the actor's job to forge a relationship, and sometimes that relationship is a tricky one. It is easy to feel resentful of actors who try to blame others for what is mostly an inadequacy in themselves. I was once directing a piece of new writing about a husband and wife. The actor playing the husband was a little self-conscious both on stage and off, and I was concerned for the actor who was playing the wife. We were both far too professional to mention anything during rehearsals, but afterwards I simply said that I thought she handled the situation well. Without either of us risking our integrity, she replied 'Oh, he was great. He gave me loads to use in my relationship with him.' She had indeed been playing the wife as particularly impatient and desperate, and the play had been well-served by her developing this relationship. Some actors have the attitude that they will use everything they are given to their advantage, and everything can be developed into an impulse to be creative.

Commitment to the truth of the imagination in the scene is another essential quality. Never come out of a scene or comment on what is happening mid-rehearsal. A total commitment allows the creativity to originate somewhere deep within you, and you will be spontaneously inventive and playful.

Smiling often reveals a need for affirmation and a lack of confidence. Like laughing, apologising or commenting, it can get in the way of the level of commitment which is required in a rehearsal. In the book *Essential Acting*, Brigid Panet explains the importance of not smiling:

> *A no-smiling run is extremely useful, especially for comedy; it is always important to break through the charm barrier which actors, often unintentionally, hide behind in their need for approval.*[1]

This 'charm' and need for approval is a mechanism which prevents the actor from fully committing to the imaginative truth of the play.

Actors who talk about how they are going to act, or make reference to their personal experiences in rehearsal, are often just wasting time. An actor's intelligence involves being able to think on their feet, and respond in an authentic manner to the imaginative truth of the situation. There is no need for an actor to talk about something, when they can simply *do it* when rehearsing the scene. Everyone in the rehearsal room generally likes this way of working. It is creative and enabling of others. If the director does not like something, he or she will simply ask you to do it differently. It is worth taking the risk. The benefits of keeping the rehearsal going, rather than stopping to talk, are clear: flow, creativity, organic growth and kinaesthetic familiarity are all effortlessly developed. After all, any information sits in the body of the actor, not simply in the mind. Time is needed to make the connection, and move from a state of abstract thinking to a state of active doing. This shift can only happen through an even and productive rehearsal period which involves the actor being active most of the time.

Use the rhythm of the rehearsal to your advantage. When energy is low, and you are rehearsing a scene that you have done several times before, use unexpected rhythms. This is especially effective if everyone has slipped into the same generalised rhythm. Make a line faster than before or slow it down; make it more direct or less direct; make it snappier or more fluid. It is ideal if you can make this new rhythm relate organically to what the character is saying. Here is a suggested process:

o   Why do I speak?

o   What is the thing the character has to have? (For example, attention, support, nurture, love, affection, provocation.)

o   What is the strategy that the character employs to get what they have to have? (For example, do they flatter the person? Do they entice them? Are they lying to them?)

o   Is this an effective or an ineffective strategy?

o   What is the rhythm and energy of the strategy? (For example, direct and heavy-handed, or light and frivolous?)

Identifying the strategy and the rhythm in this way is not dependent on jargon such as 'intentions', 'activities' or 'action words'; it is a simple question concerning what the character *has to have* and what the *strategies* are. It is a pragmatic and easy approach.

There are some actors who appear to be masterful with rhythms. The energy seems to pick up onstage, and everyone seems to be relating to each other better. This new and unexpected energy can unleash a new creativity and playfulness in which all the actors experience something new. There is no need to explain that you did that old rhythmic trick – simply allow everyone to enjoy their new-found creativity.

Another challenge of the rehearsal room is about understanding the aesthetic, tone and texture of the performance. Here are some questions to ask yourself:

o Is this realism? If so, how emotionally available do I need to be? Do I contain the emotion or reveal it more fully?

o What size of acting is appropriate? Do I keep the acting close, or allow a larger scale?

o What is the style of the comedy? Is it heightened? Is there buffoonery? Or is the comedy realistic?

o Is the blocking set in stone, or is there room for improvisation?

o Do the other actors welcome spontaneity and inventiveness, or do I have to be absolutely consistent each time?

This is all a matter of developing an appropriate taste for the style of the rehearsal and the performance. Careful observation of the way the rehearsals are progressing – and paying close attention to the director's notes – are the ways to understand the overall taste. You should act within the parameters of this.

Trust and compliance are also essential qualities for the rehearsal room. Trust what the director is asking you to do and comply swiftly and gently. If the rehearsal process is causing feelings of anxiety or vulnerability, try and take some time to reflect on why:

o   Are you uncertain about your acting?

o   Do you have a different artistic sensibility?

o   Do you feel that your point of view is not being heard?

o   Are the director or other cast members being unreasonable?

With the first two of these points, you must simply deal with it, regrettably. Discussion will often only hinder progress, and irritate others in the company. It is important to appreciate that this is probably your own personal neurosis, and has little to do with anyone else. Regarding the third point, when you feel that you are not being heard, see if you can translate your suggestions into your practical work. Rather than *discuss* what you want to do, why not just *do* it? If the director does not think that it is an effective suggestion, you will be advised of this, and then you simply do it differently the next time. This is all part of developing an actor's intelligence; the type of intelligence which begins and ends in the body.

Exercise: What does an actor look like?

- Take some time to sit quietly and write out the qualities that you consider a successful actor to have.

- Now take some time to write out the qualities that you consider a diva or a star to have.

- Compare your lists and ask yourself which you would prefer to be, and which attitudes you show in reality.

Don't move on until you have done this. Actually write the list down, don't just do it in your head.

Here are our suggested lists:

A successful actor is	A diva's attitude consists of
Punctual	Self-centred
Open	Defensive
Compliant	Resistant
Willing	Difficult
Receptive	Passive-aggressive
Emotionally available	Obstinate
Playful	Rigid
Appreciative	Vain
Graceful	Spiky
Supportive	Isolated
Full of humility	Judgemental

Do you dare to ask someone who was involved with your last rehearsal process which of the qualities you showed most of? Were you perhaps a little bit of a diva?

In *The Art of Possibility*, Rosamund and Benjamin Zander explain a simple technique to enhance harmony and collaboration in any group: imagine that you are awarding grades, as if at school or college, and give everyone an 'A' – they have all deserved it.[2] This immediately changes your attitude to everyone in the room. Everyone is doing their best, and everyone is focusing to the degree that they are able. This makes all mistakes, clumsiness and awkwardness understandable. Everyone is doing their best. We are all human and we are all trying our best to get it right, despite our fallibility. Scorn, disapproval or harshness become redundant when you understand that everyone deserves an 'A'. Glynn MacDonald, an associate at Shakespeare's Globe Theatre and winner of the 2011 Sam Wanamaker Award, has a phrase that she sometimes uses when the atmosphere is getting tense in rehearsal: 'We're all doing the best we can,' and then she adds, with a wry smile, 'it's just that our "bests" vary.' This attitude is a way of simply allowing others to be, without fear of judgement.

The one ingredient I bring to all of my films is the ability to listen to anybody who has a good idea on the production. I'm very collaborative with actors, with my writers, with my editor, my cinematographer, with Johnny Williams who does all of my scores. And I just think from a very young age my parents taught me probably the most valuable lesson of my life – sometimes it's better not to talk, but to listen.

Steven Spielberg

Summary

The attitude of a successful actor concerns bringing joy into the rehearsal room, and into the job. There will be times during rehearsal when the process is overwhelming and you are not enjoying yourself. It requires a maturity and healthy approach to understand that this is part of the process of organic growth, and that even if it appears overwhelming, it is still a joyous experience.

1   Brigid Panet, *Essential Acting* (Routledge, 2009)

2   Rosamund Stone Zander and Benjamin Zander, *The Art of Possibility* (Penguin, 2006)

A Final Thought

Now, at the end of this book, there is a chance that you will have come full circle. You will have conquered your sense of defeat, defined your reasons to act, developed yourself as a brand and a business, and understood how to present yourself professionally. You will, also, hopefully have got some work which will have been fulfilling and rewarding. However, when the work comes to an end, you may find yourself alone, feeling lost and disenfranchised once again. The cycle of looking for work and going to auditions begins again. This brings us to the point that the practices in this book are not something that you do once to get you out of a slump, but something to which you return again and again to maintain the sense of well-being and self-belief that will sustain you throughout your career. Indeed, this is the work, and it is a job that you have to do daily. Containing your thoughts within a mental structure that enables opportunity is your duty. You have the choice to remain positive, connected and creative.

We could finish by wishing you luck. But as you know by now, we think that we all make our own luck. So, instead we will finish by wishing you positivity and healthy action. May it lead to good fortune because – as we all know – fortune favours the brave.

Appendices

Useful Online Resources

A

www.artsjobs.org.uk

This free website has useful information for people who work in all areas of the arts. There is a free weekly email service also.

www.thestage.co.uk

There is plenty of the newspaper's content online, including some jobs and audition news, and also announcements of what plays and films are is going into production.

www.spotlight.com

This subscription website is key in finding actors for agents, casting directors and directors. You must qualify to register. Spotlight also offers workshops and other services.

www.uk.castingcallpro.com

This subscription website is a place for directors, producers and casting directors to advertise auditions and potential jobs. Mostly student films, fringe theatre and profit–share are to be found.

www.castingnow.co.uk and **www.castweb.co.uk**

These subscription websites are similar in content and style to Casting Call Pro.

www.mandy.com and **www.shootingpeople.org**

While these websites are generally for people who crew films, there are jobs for actors advertised now and again.

www.virginmediashorts.co.uk and **www.bbc.co.uk/filmnetwork**

These websites give a good idea (and hopefully inspiration) of what short films are being made.

www.shortfilmdepot.com and **www.withoutabox.com**

Once you have made your short film, these are the websites to use to get included in short-film festivals.

www.whatsonstage.com and **www.londontheatre.co.uk**

Both these websites are full of news, reviews and offers. They also announce what plays are coming up soon.

www.britishtheatreguide.info

This website is full of news and reviews. It also announces the future seasons of regional theatres.

www.tkts.co.uk

This is the website of the half-price ticket booth in Leicester Square in London. It is run by the Society of London Theatres. You can see what is available and how much it is going to cost before you go to Leicester Square and queue.

www.attitude4acting.co.uk

You can get in touch with Andrew and Tara on their website. Leave messages on the discussion forums and gather information. They can also be contacted via Twitter (@attitude4acting) and Facebook (http://tinyurl.com/6xjktmu).

It is recommended that you examine the content of the websites thoroughly and read the terms and conditions before you decide to subscribe.

B Headshots, Showreels and Letters

Headshots

- In the UK, black-and-white prints rather than colour are still preferable.

- When choosing a photographer, have a good look through Spotlight or Contacts, and choose someone whose style you like.

- Meet the photographer before you book them for the shoot, so that you are sure that you get on well with them and you feel relaxed around each other.

- You must look like yourself in the photographs, rather than an *idealised* version of yourself.

- When choosing photographs from the contact sheet, seek plenty of advice, but beware – your close friends and family are not always the best people to ask.

- Always choose a shot in which you are looking directly at the camera. The three-quarters profile shots are not suitable, no matter how stylish.

- Be careful with the framing of the photograph – simple, centred framing is preferable.

o   Be aware of trends. For example, tinting was popular a few years ago; actors had headshots printed with a slightly yellow or slightly blue tint. This is to be avoided.

o   Know whether you are most comfortable doing a studio shoot or an outside shoot. They can produce equally good results.

o   Have a solid understanding of your casting and ensure that your choices of photograph support the full possibilities of your casting type.

Showreels

o   Keep in mind that the person watching the showreel may only watch the first twenty or thirty seconds, so edit your showreel accordingly.

o   You will be assessed on your look and how you appear on camera, rather than on the quality of your acting.

o   Keep the showreel fast-moving – lots of reaction shots are preferable to showing whole scenes.

o   Make sure your name and contact details appear often (either intermittently or constantly) on screen.

o   Understand the potential (and limitations) of your casting for acting on screen, and ensure the showreel reflects this.

o   Choose mainly close-up shots with a variety of tone: lighter, darker, dramatic, comic.

o   Background music with a 'Creative Commons' licence can easily be found online if you are worried about infringing copyright – this is a concern if you are going to upload your showreel to a website.

o   If dialogue is important in the clip, make sure that the sound quality is clear.

o   Be wary – an amateur-looking showreel will look worse than not having a showreel at all.

Writing Letters

o   Be concise.

o   Be clear about what you want.

o   Be clear about what you are offering.

o   Always appear professional in a letter or email – you are representing your business.

o   Avoid an over-polite, aspirational tone: 'I would really appreciate...' or 'I would very much like to arrange a meeting...'

o   A 'quirky' letter does not always help you to stand out from the crowd in a positive way.

o   Approaching people in letters does get results, but you may have to write hundreds of letters to see these results.

o   Be clear about the professional work you have done, and the reviews you have received and why you are 'bankable'.

o   Always name-check a mutual contact, but get permission first: 'Joe Bloggs suggested I drop you a line...'

o   Know when to appear formal, and when to appear casual – getting the wrong register could be seen as a faux-pas.

o   Do not lie or exaggerate; for example, working as an extra is not the same as being cast in a role in a film – even if the director was Steven Spielberg.

Further Reading

C

Brown, Swart & Meyler, *Emotional Intelligence* (*Neuroleadership Journal*, 2009)

Callow, Simon, *Being an Actor* (Vintage, 2004)

Covey, Stephen R., *The Seven Habits of Highly Effective People* (Simon and Schuster, 2004)

Denny, Richard, *Selling to Win* (Kogan Page, 2009)

Ferrazzi, Keith, *Never Eat Alone* (Doubleday Business, 2005)

Ferrucci, Piero, *What We May Be: Techniques for Psychological and Spiritual Growth* (Jeremy P. Tarcher, 2000)

Gallwey, W. Timothy, *The Inner Game of Tennis* (Pan Books, 1986)

Gladwell, Malcolm, *The Tipping Point* (Abacus, 2001)

Johnson, Spencer, *Who Moved My Cheese?* (Vermilion, 1999)

Panet, Brigid, *Essential Acting* (Routledge, 2009)

Robinson, Ken with Lou Aronica, *The Element: How Finding Your Passion Changes Everything* (Allen Lane, 2009)

West, Timothy and Prunella Scales, *So You Want To Be An Actor?* (Nick Hern Books, 2005)

Wiseman, Richard, *59 Seconds* (Pan, 2010)

Zaffron, Steve and Dave Logan, *The Three Laws of Performance* (Jossey Bass, 2009)

Zander, Rosamund Stone and Benjamin Zander, *The Art of Possibility: Transforming Professional and Personal Life* (Penguin, 2006)

Quotations taken from existing interviews are from the following sources:

p. 12   Tamsin Grieg in the *Independent*, Saturday 6th May 2006, 'Tamsin Greig: Green Goddess' by Nick Duerden

p. 39   Sally Hawkins in the *Guardian*, Friday 11th April 2008, 'Lady Luck' by Maddy Costa

p. 42   Bill Nighy in the *Observer*, Sunday 31st October 2004, 'Something of the Nighy' by Miranda Sawyer

p. 65   Maxine Peake in the *Guardian*, Saturday 15th May 2010, 'Maxine Peake: The Misfit' by Amanda Mitchison

p. 131   Damian Lewis in the *Daily Telegraph*, Monday 18th April 2011, 'Damian Lewis Interview' by John Preston

p. 141   Emma Thompson in the *Observer*, Sunday 16th October 2005, 'Warts 'n' all' by Kate Kellaway